WordPress

for the Technically Challenged

Book 5 in the Internet Marketing FAST series

Copyright and Enquiries

Comments or enquiries may be left in the *Contact Me* page at:

https://superaffiliatechallenge.com/contact-me/

Contents

Copyright and Enquiries 2

WordPress..9

Hosting Your Site 9

   Pointing Your Domain Name to Your Host's DNS 9

      Sign into Namecheap 10

      Select the Domain to be Updated 11

      Enter Your Web Host's Name Servers...................................12

      Save and Propagate...14

Installing WordPress..15

Modifying the Basic Setup 17

   Trash the Default Post and Page 17

   Fix Site Identity 18

   Clean up the Plugins..19

      Activate the All in One SEO Pack 20

      Leave the Classic Editor activated..22

      Delete the EWWW Image Optimizer. 22

Install Backup and Restore 22

   All in One WP Migration 23

   Create Your First Backup 24

Creating a Logo 26

Installing Thrive..26

   The Thrive Product Manager...26

   Install a Thrive Theme and Thrive Architect..............................29

   Clean up the Themes..30

   Customizations 32

      Theme Options...33

      Performance 33

      Set up Your Logo...34

      Footer Copyright Links 35

WordPress

for the Technically Challenged

Style and Layout Settings 35

Blog Settings 37

Set Logo Size 39

Protecting Email Addresses 41

Adding a New User to Your WordPress Site 42

Select Add New 43

Complete the Add New User Form 44

Add the New User 45

Check the WordPress Email 47

Log in with the New User's Credentials 49

The New User Is Logged in 51

Adding Required Pages and Posts 51

Privacy Policy 52

Affiliate Disclosure 56

Articles 56

The Post List Element 57

About (Me) 62

Contact (Me) 68

Creating Your Menus 70

Your WordPress Site Is Ready! 75

Other Plugins 75

All-in-One SEO Pack 77

All-in-One WP Migration 77

Monster Insights 77

Under Construction 77

Smart Slider 3 78

AliDropship 78

WordPress

for the Technically Challenged

The Rest of the Books..80

Available Now 80

Not Yet Available...80

About the Author..82

WordPress

for the Technically Challenged

Table of Figures

Figure 1: Log in to Namecheap 10

Figure 2: Click on Domain List 11

Figure 3: Select the Domain Name to be Updated 12

Figure 4: Click on Websites 13

Figure 5: Your Website's SiteGround Name Servers 13

Figure 6: Update the Name Servers 14

Figure 7: Add New Website 15

Figure 8: Enter Your Domain Name 16

Figure 9: Trash the Default Post 17

Figure 10: Trash the Default Pages 18

Figure 11: Click on Customize 19

Figure 12: Initial Plugin Setup 20

Figure 13: Activate XML Sitemap 21

Figure 14: Plugins Updated 22

Figure 15: Install All in One WP Migration 23

Figure 16: Backup Tool in WP Menu 24

Figure 17: Select the Backup's Destination 25

Figure 18: Install Thrive Product Manager 27

Figure 19: Thrive Product Manager Video 28

Figure 20: Select the Plugins and Themes to Install 29

Figure 21: Click on Themes 30

Figure 22: Activate the New Theme 31

Figure 23: Confirm Theme Deletion 32

Figure 24: Thrive Theme Options 33

Figure 25: Performance 34

Figure 26: Style and Layout Settings 36

Figure 27: Blog Settings 38

Figure 28: Analytics and Scripts 39

Figure 29: Customize Logo Width 40

WordPress

for the Technically Challenged

Figure 30: Install Email Encoder 42

Figure 31: Select Add New 43

Figure 32: Add New User Form 44

Figure 33: The Completed Add New User Form 45

Figure 34: Save the Generated Password 46

Figure 35: New User Created 47

Figure 36: Password Email 48

Figure 37: Password Reset from Email 49

Figure 38: Log in as the New User 50

Figure 39: Logged in as the New User 51

Figure 40: Click on Add New (Page) 52

Figure 41: Launch Thrive Architect 53

Figure 42: Add a Thrive Architect Text Element 54

Figure 43: Privacy Policy Pasted into Text Box 55

Figure 44: Publish the Page 56

Figure 45: The Post List Element 57

Figure 46: Post List Element Added to Articles Page 58

Figure 47: Post List Design 59

Figure 48: Filter Posts 60

Figure 49: Select the Posts to be Displayed 60

Figure 50: The Finished Articles Page 61

Figure 51: Click the Add New (Post) Button 62

Figure 52: Add New Category 63

Figure 53: Select the Image Element 64

Figure 54: Set the Image Properties 66

Figure 55: About Me Page with Placeholder Text 67

Figure 56: Contact (Me) Post 69

Figure 57: Select Appearance then Menus 70

Figure 58: Create Your Header Menu 70

Figure 59: Set Location to Primary Menu 71

WordPress

for the Technically Challenged

Figure 60: Create the Home Menu Item 72
Figure 61: Change the Menu Item Name to Upper Case 73
Figure 62: Select Create a New Menu 74
Figure 63: Select Footer Menu as the Location 74
Figure 64: Add a New Plugin 76
Figure 65: Search for the Plugin You Want 76
Figure 66: Install and Activate the New Plugin 77
Figure 67: Under Construction Enabled 78

WordPress

WordPress is arguably the best, easiest and most effective platform to build a commercial website on.

What used to be incredibly difficult has been made a lot easier with WordPress.

But many people still struggle with it.

Much of its strength comes from the huge number of themes and plugins that have been created to extend its functionality. Some are free. Many are not. They don't all co-exist peacefully. Some used to be good, but haven't been updated to work with later versions of WordPress. It's a bit of a minefield.

This guide will lead you through installing a basic WordPress site and turning it into an attractive front for your prospective business.

I can't possibly cover all of the variables inherent in all the different domain name hosts, web hosts, themes and plugins that are available. All of the examples used in this document are based on our recommendations. Namecheap for domain name hosting, SiteGround for web hosting and Thrive for themes and plugins.

Hosting Your Site

Pointing Your Domain Name to Your Host's DNS

When someone enters your domain name into a web browser like Google or Bing, it has to find your web host to bring up your website. Your web host and your domain name host must be linked.

WordPress

This is achieved by entering your web host's DNS (Domain Name Servers) into your domain name details at your domain name host's website. This is a one-time job.

If you used Namecheap as recommended for your domain name host, this is how you do it.

Sign into Namecheap
Sign into Namecheap.

Figure 1: Log in to Namecheap

Then click on *Domain List*.

WordPress

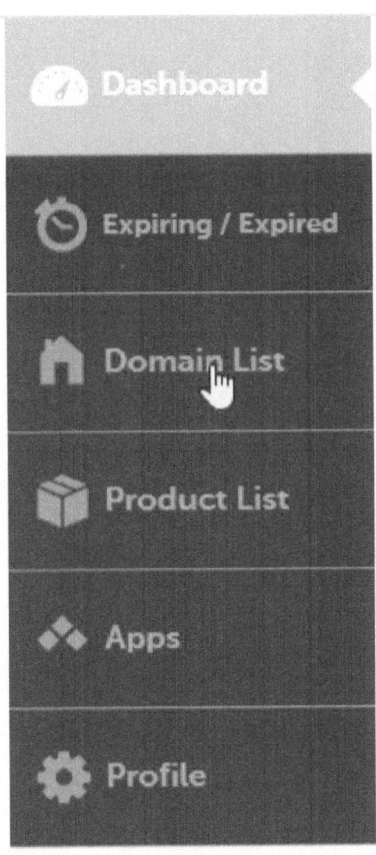

Figure 2: Click on Domain List

Select the Domain to be Updated

Click the check box next to the domain name to be edited then the drop-down labelled *Actions* and select *DNS / Host Records*.

WordPress
for the Technically Challenged

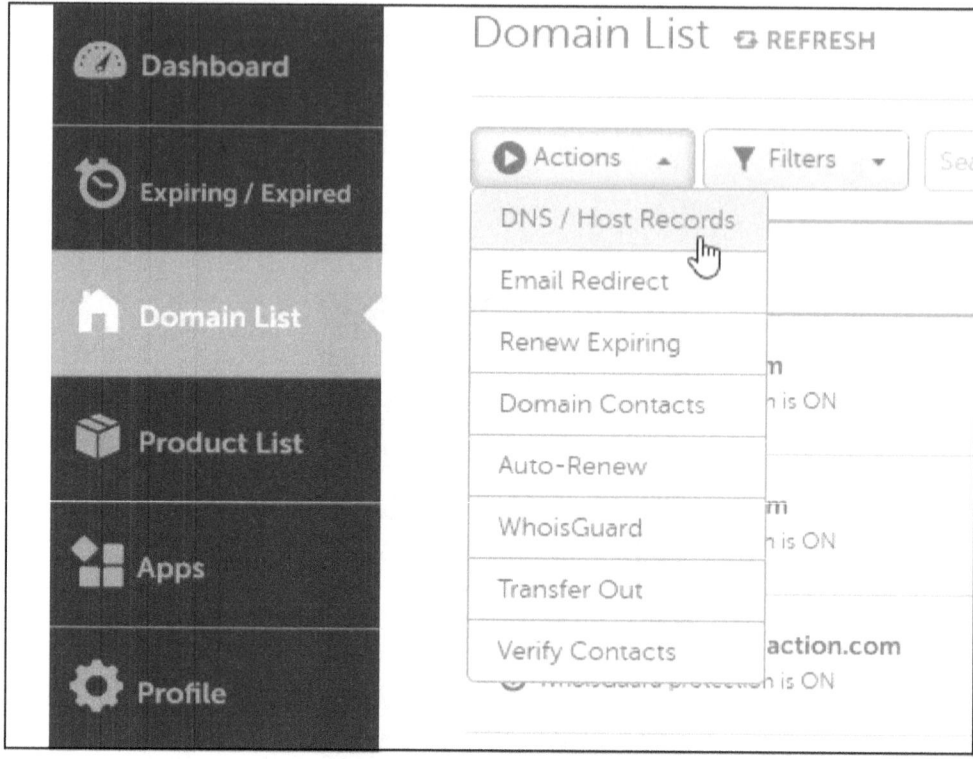

Figure 3: Select the Domain Name to be Updated

On the next screen, click the check boxes that say you know what you're doing and then the **Next** button.

Enter Your Web Host's Name Servers

Check the radio button Custom DNS and enter your web host's domain name servers. If you are using my recommended SiteGround as your web host, they will have advised you of the correct domain name servers to use.

If you're not sure of SiteGround's name servers, just log in to your account there and click on Websites.

WordPress
for the Technically Challenged

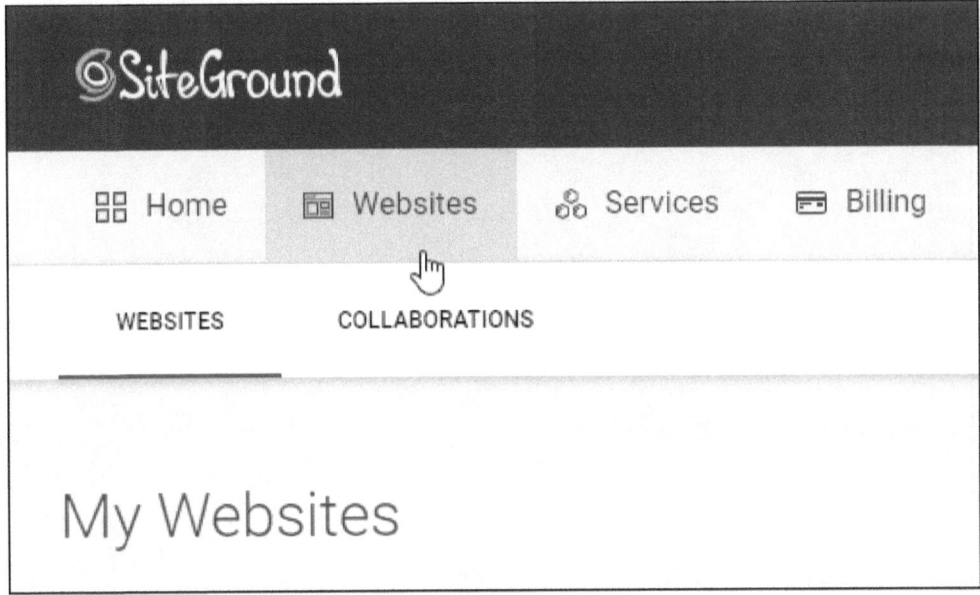

Figure 4: Click on Websites

Click the **Site Tools** button for your website and it will show you the site's domain name servers.

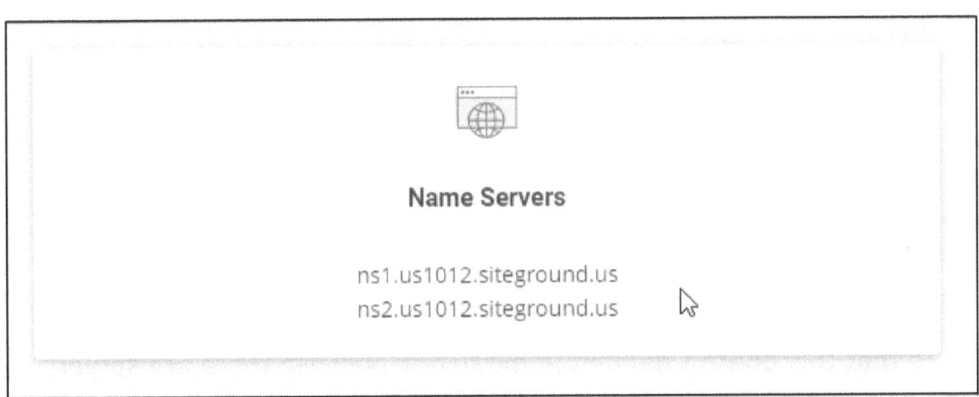

Figure 5: Your Website's SiteGround Name Servers

WordPress

for the Technically Challenged

Then you can update the domain name servers (DNS) at your domain name host.

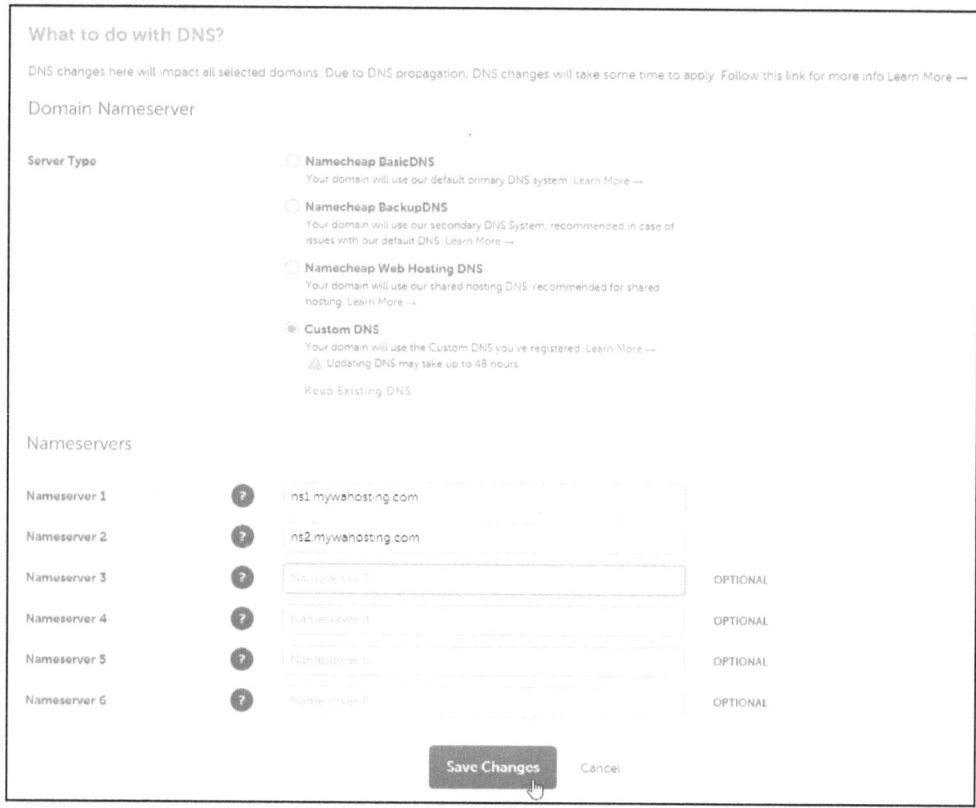

Figure 6: Update the Name Servers

Save and Propagate

Then click on *Save Changes*.

Note that this doesn't happen immediately because there are servers all over the world that need to be updated. This is called propagation. Although you will be told to allow up to 48 hours, it normally only takes a few hours.

WordPress

After a little while, you will be able to install WordPress at your web host.

If you are not using Namecheap as your domain name host, the procedure will be different, but the principle is the same. Similarly, if you are not using SiteGround as your web host, the name servers will also be different.

Installing WordPress

Log in to your SiteGround account and click the **New Website** button. This will take you to the *Add New Website* page.

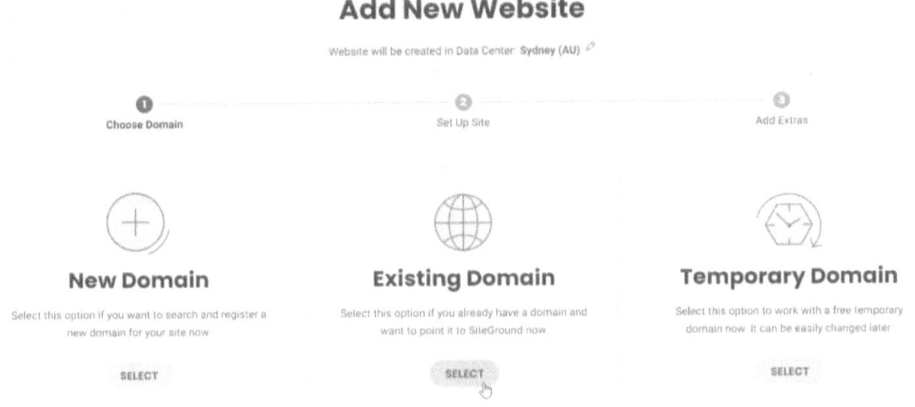

Figure 7: Add New Website

Under *Existing Domain*, click the **Select** button.

WordPress
for the Technically Challenged

Enter Your Domain Name

yourdomain.com

CONTINUE

Figure 8: Enter Your Domain Name

Then, enter the domain name you registered with Namecheap and click on the **Continue** button.

All we want to do with the next screen is to create an empty WordPress website.

Click the **Skip and Create Empty Site** button.

There's no need to Add the Site Scanner option.

Simply click the **Finish** button and your new WordPress site will be created. How easy is that!

16

WordPress

for the Technically Challenged

Modifying the Basic Setup

There are a couple of things you should do to modify the basic WordPress setup.

Trash the Default Post and Page

In your site's WordPress back office, click on *Posts*. You will see the default WordPress post "Hello world!".

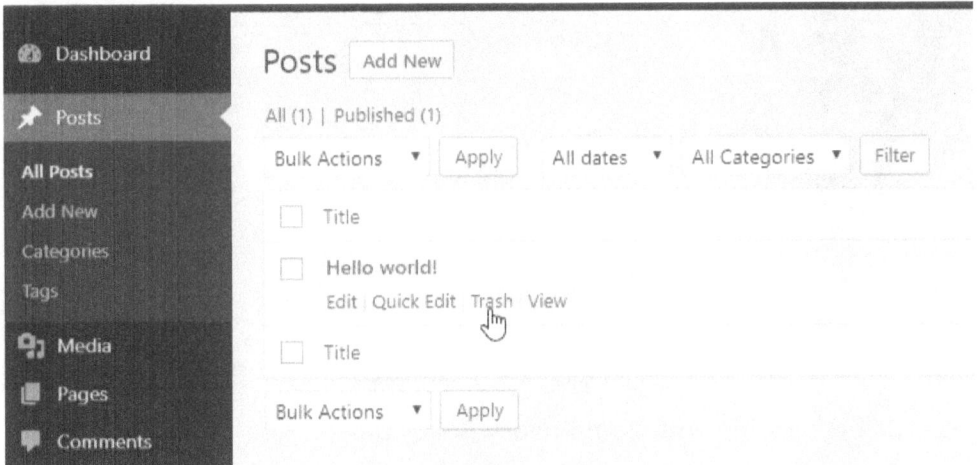

Figure 9: Trash the Default Post

Hover over the default post and click on *Trash*.

In your site's WordPress back office, click on *Pages*. You will see the default WordPress pages "Privacy Policy" and "Sample Page".

WordPress
for the Technically Challenged

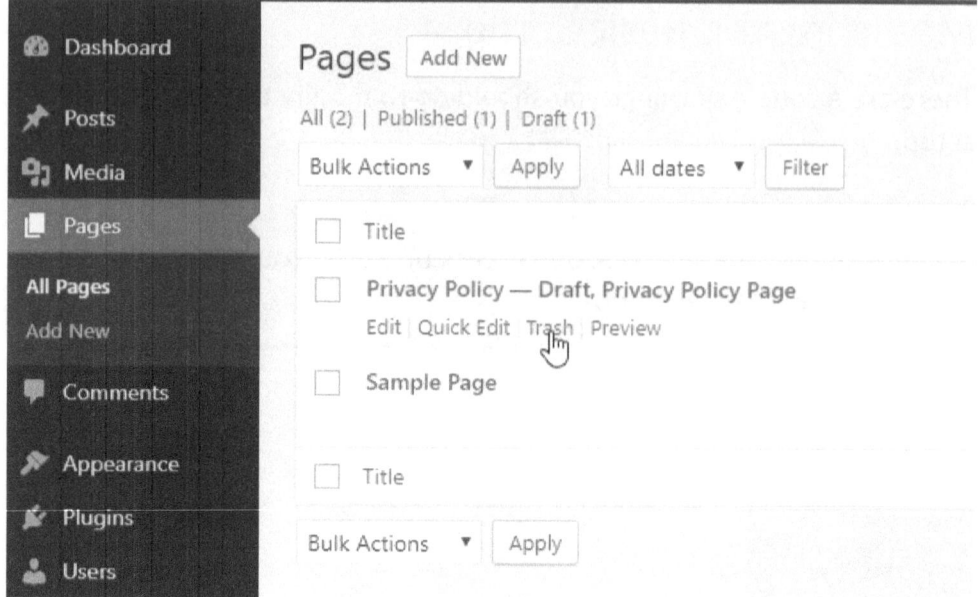

Figure 10: Trash the Default Pages

Hover over each of the default pages in turn and click on *Trash*.

You will be creating your own Privacy Policy page later.

Fix Site Identity

In the WordPress back office, click on *Appearance* then *Customize*.

WordPress

for the Technically Challenged

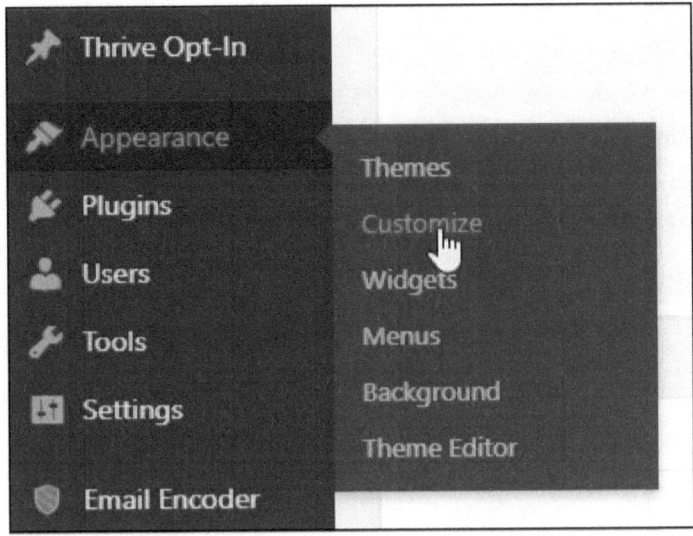

Figure 11: Click on Customize

Select Site Identity and complete Site Title and Tagline as appropriate for your site. You can always change these later.

Then click on the **Publish** button.

Clean up the Plugins

In the WordPress back office, click on *Plugins*.

WordPress
for the Technically Challenged

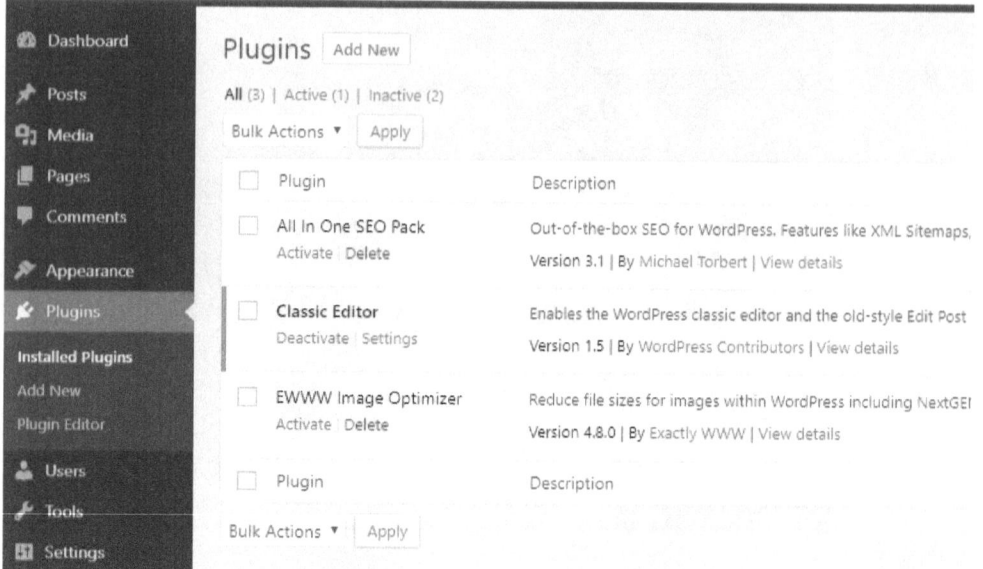

Figure 12: Initial Plugin Setup

Activate the All in One SEO Pack

If you've followed my recommendation and are hosting your site with Wealthy Affiliate, the All in One SEO Pack plugin is pre-installed. It's an excellent plugin. Click *Activate* and then make the following adjustments:

Under All-in-One SEO, click on *Feature Manager* and activate the XML Sitemap.

WordPress

for the Technically Challenged

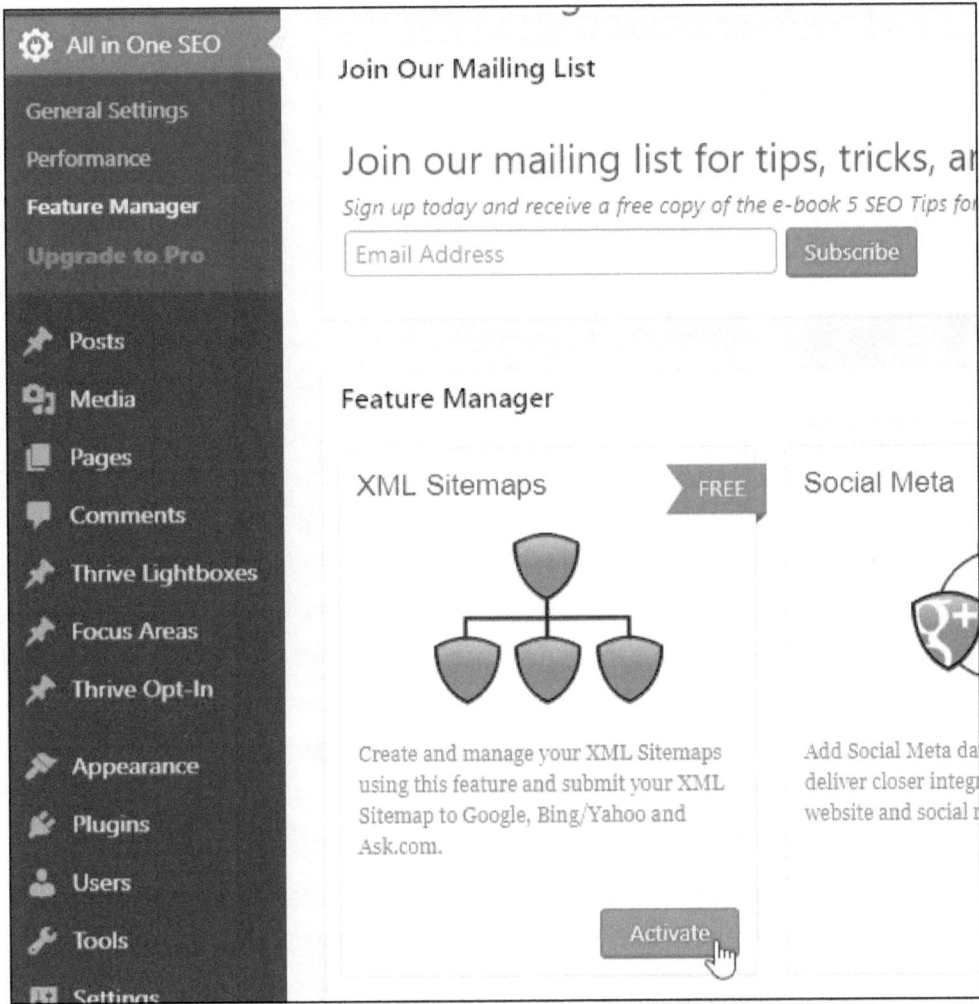

Figure 13: Activate XML Sitemap

There is no need to upgrade to the Pro version of All in One SEO Pack. The free version gives us all you need.

Leave the Classic Editor activated.

Delete the EWWW Image Optimizer.

If you've followed my recommendation to get Thrive Themes and Plugins, you can delete the EWWW Image Optimizer as Thrive has a better one.

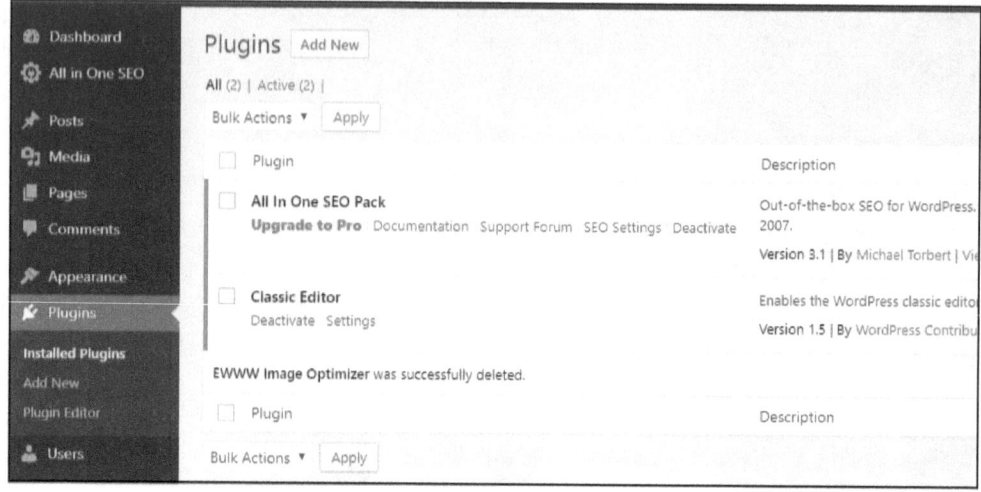

Figure 14: Plugins Updated

Install Backup and Restore

Most web hosts back up their hosted sites on a regular basis, typically daily. You don't see the backup; it's kept on their servers.

There are three reasons you shouldn't rely on that backup and need your own local one as well.

- The timing isn't under your control. If you've just put in several hours of painstaking work on your website that would be devastating to lose, you'll feel much better if you back it up immediately.

- Having your own backup means you can move to another web host easily if you wish. Just point the domain name at the new host, create an empty WordPress site and restore your backup file to it.
- What if you have an issue with your existing host? Financial, for example. Without your own backup, your host can hold your website to ransom. Particularly if they also host your domain name. With a local backup and your domain name hosted elsewhere, they have no control over you.

All in One WP Migration

There are several backup and restore plugins for WordPress. I recommend *All in One WP Migration* because I've used it to back up *and* restore several websites and I know that it works.

Click on Plugins >> Add New and then do a keyword search for *All in One WP Migration*.

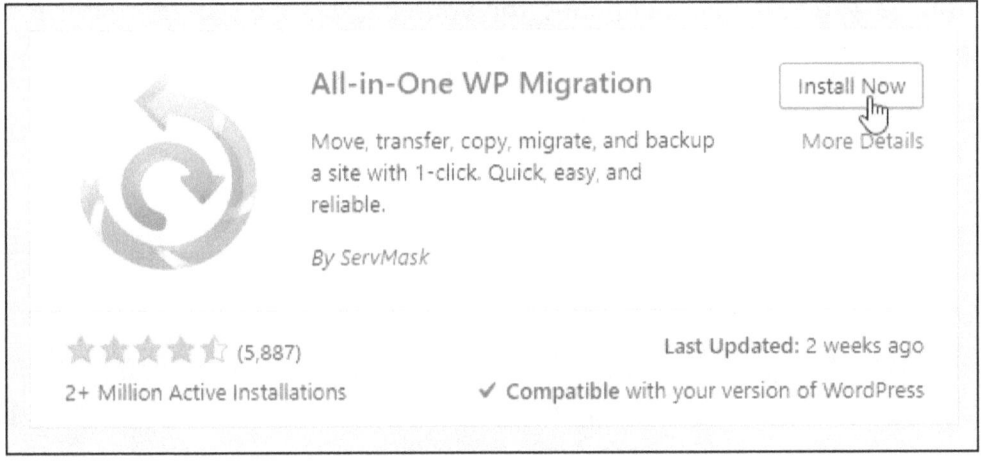

Figure 15: Install All in One WP Migration

Install the plugin and then Activate it.

WordPress

for the Technically Challenged

Create Your First Backup

Once you've activated the plugin, it will appear as a new tool in the WordPress menu.

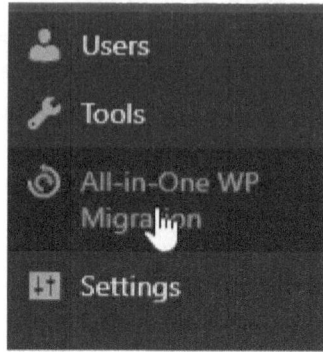

Figure 16: Backup Tool in WP Menu

Click on the menu item and then *Export* to create your first backup.

You have a number of options for your backup file's destination. My preference is as a file on my local computer.

WordPress

for the Technically Challenged

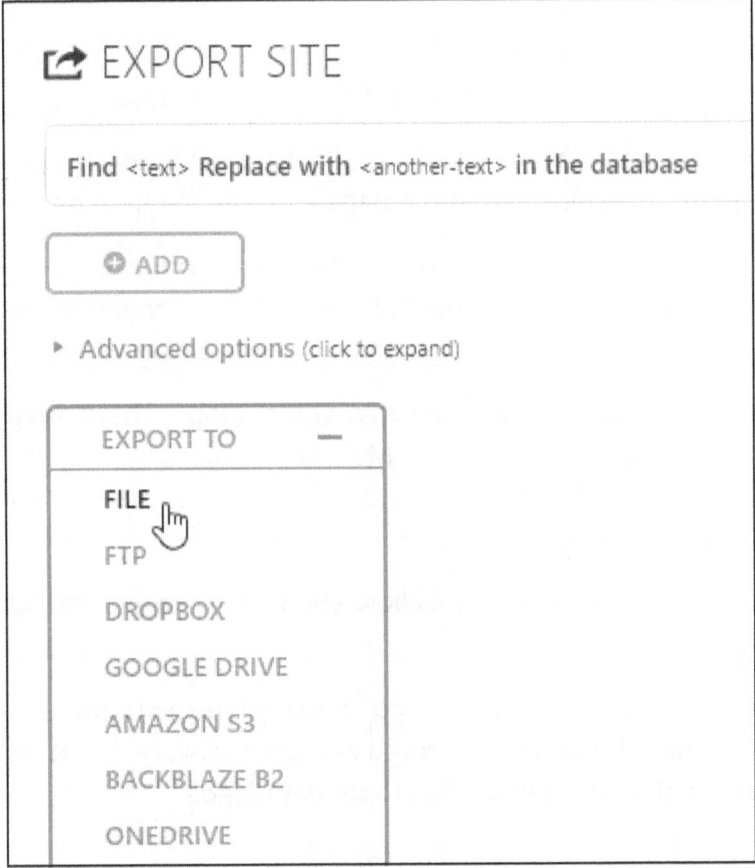

Figure 17: Select the Backup's Destination

Progress messages are displayed as the backup takes place, followed by a flashing invitation to download the file.

Click on the invitation and the backup file is downloaded into your Downloads folder, from where you can copy it to wherever you want to keep it permanently.

WordPress

Creating a Logo

An attractive logo is an important part of your site's impact.

You can have a small logo, with your menu to the right or (my preference) a banner logo, spreading across the page with the menu underneath.

You can get either designed for a reasonable price at Fiverr (go to https://www.fiverr.com/ and search for logo design) or you can make your own.

You will need to find a suitable uncopyrighted image. There are a number of sites that provide these. My personal favorite is Pixabay (https://pixabay.com/). Their image quality is excellent and I can always find one that is suitable.

Then you need software that will allow you to trim, resize and add text to create your actual logo.

A tool that I've used for years and wouldn't be without is Snagit by Techsmith. Snagit is the king of screen capture software, but it also comes with an editor that you can use to create your logo.

Installing Thrive

Thrive make it particularly easy to install their themes and plugins. You install one plugin, called the Thrive Product Manager and then use it to install other Thrive themes and plugins.

The Thrive Product Manager

To get it, log into Thrive and go to *Access Your Products*.

WordPress

for the Technically Challenged

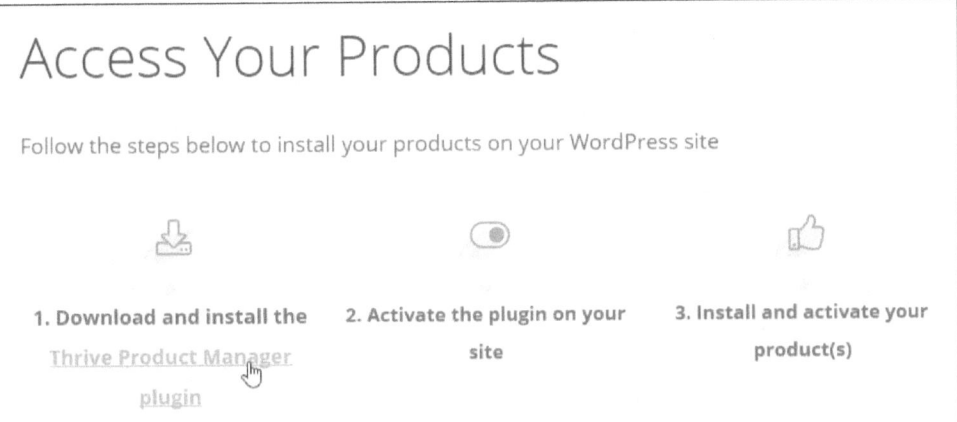

Figure 18: Install Thrive Product Manager

You only need one plugin. It's called thrive-product-manager.zip and you'll be given access to it when you purchase Thrive Themes. Install it as you would any other plugin.

That is, download its zip file to somewhere on your local hard disk (I use a plugins sub-folder under Documents) then in your WordPress back office, go to Plugins >> Add New then click on the **Upload Plugin** button. Click the **Choose File** button and select the downloaded zip file.

Click the **Install Now** button and activate the plugin once it's installed.

The Thrive Product Manager allows you to install any or all of the Thrive Themes and Plugins.

WordPress

for the Technically Challenged

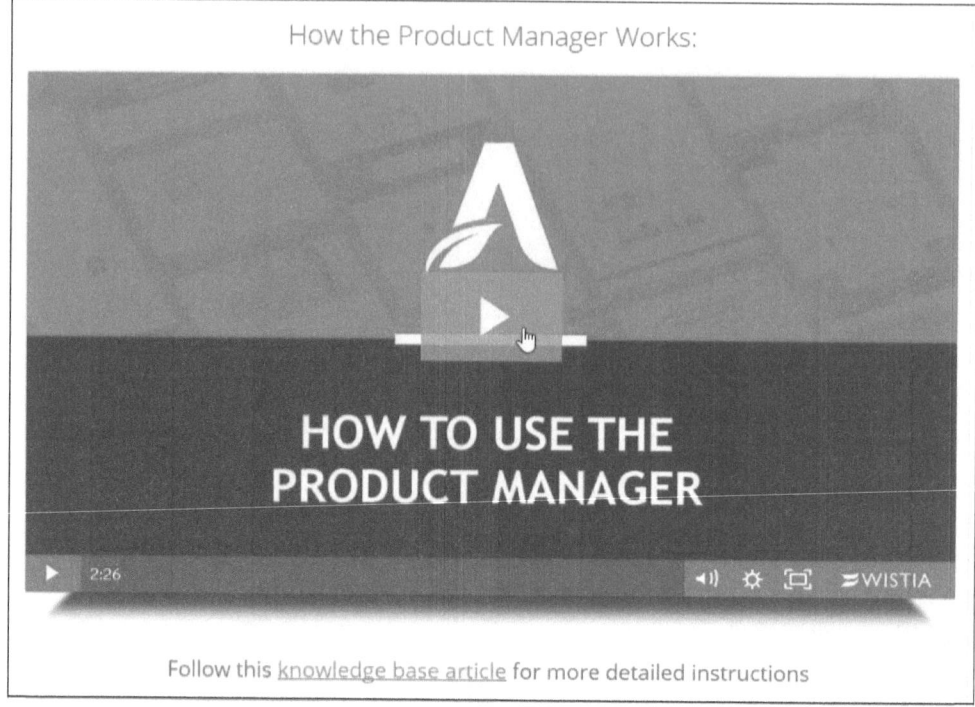

Figure 19: Thrive Product Manager Video

There's even a video explaining how to install and use the plugin.

Click on *Product Manager* in the main WP Menu and then log in to Thrive Themes with the username and password you created when you purchased.

WordPress

for the Technically Challenged

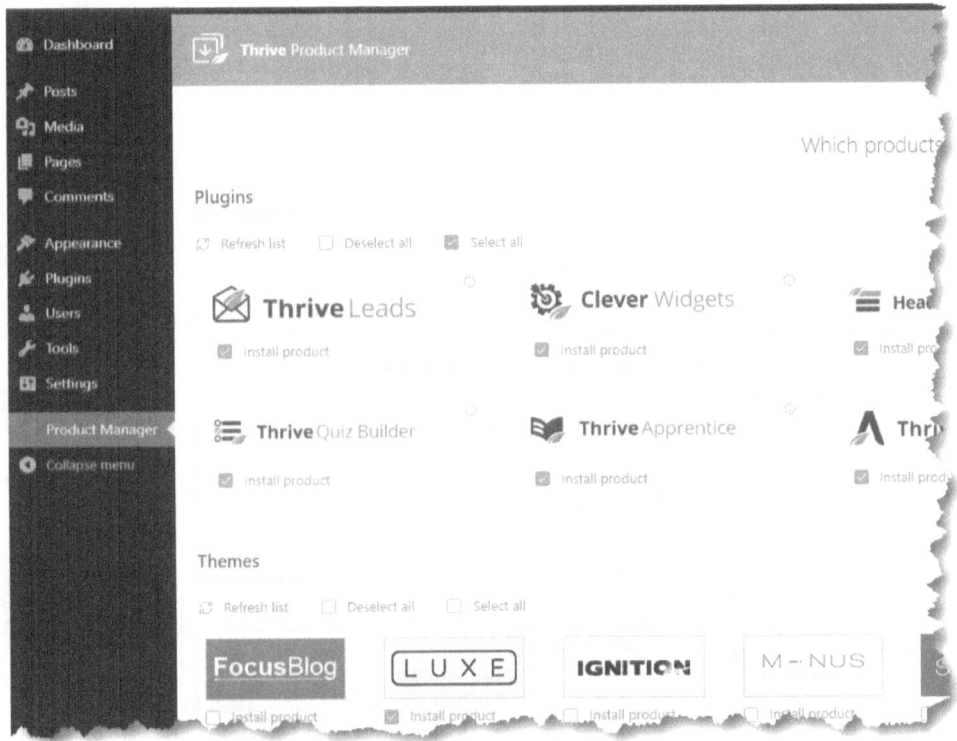

Figure 20: Select the Plugins and Themes to Install

You are shown all of the Thrive plugins and themes that are available.

Select the ones you want to install and click *Install Selected Products*.

You don't need to install everything at once. You can come back any time you want and install more.

Install a Thrive Theme and Thrive Architect

Thrive has a very powerful theme builder called Shapeshift. It deserves a user guide all by itself and I will be producing one.

WordPress

In the meantime, I suggest one of the legacy themes (just click on the + button next to Legacy Themes) and select one theme (I normally use Luxe or Rise) plus Thrive Architect. They are all you need to start building out an attractive website. In these examples, I'll assume Luxe has been selected. It creates a nice clean look.

Clean up the Themes

Now you should activate the Luxe theme and delete the now unnecessary themes that WordPress installed automatically.

In the WordPress back office, hover over *Appearance* then click on *Themes*.

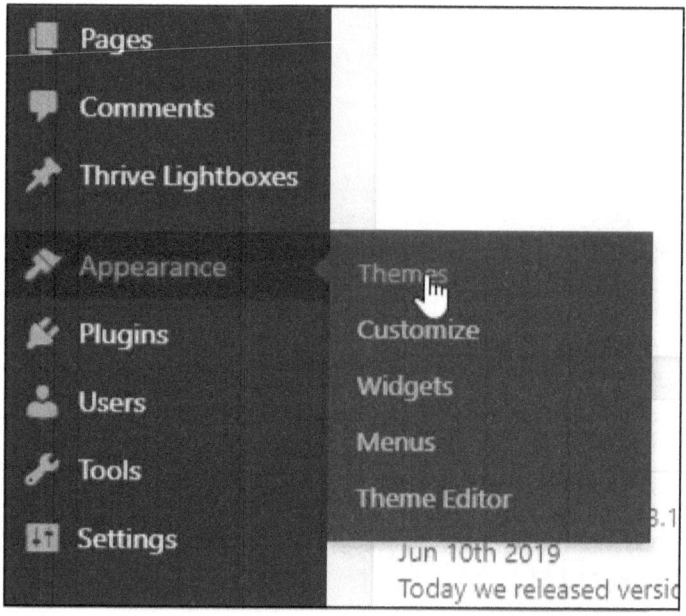

Figure 21: Click on Themes

Find the new Luxe theme and click on *Activate*.

WordPress

for the Technically Challenged

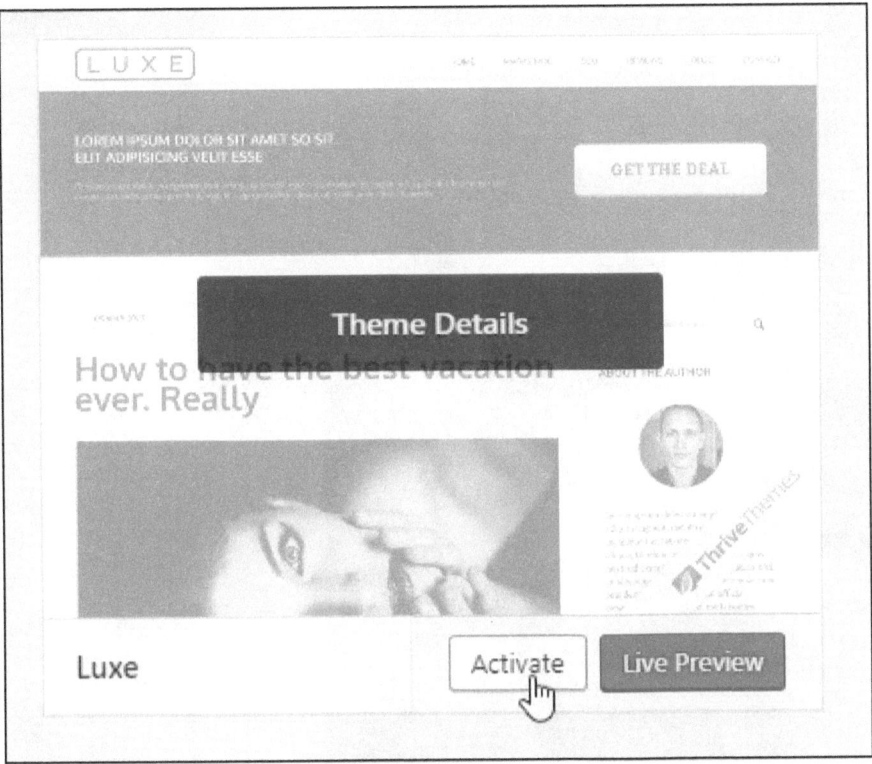

Figure 22: Activate the New Theme

Then delete all the other themes. You do this by clicking on the theme, selecting *Delete* and then confirming the deletion.

This makes you site leaner. It uses less memory and loads faster.

WordPress

for the Technically Challenged

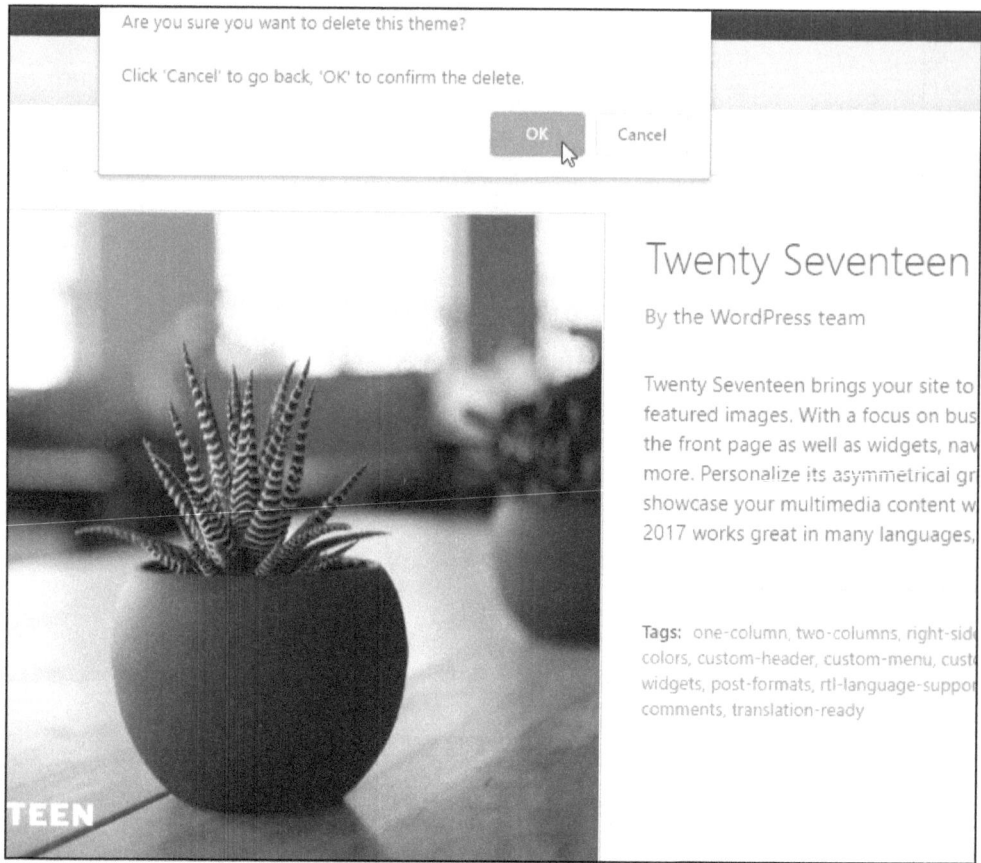

Figure 23: Confirm Theme Deletion

Customizations

Make these customizations next.

WordPress

for the Technically Challenged

Theme Options

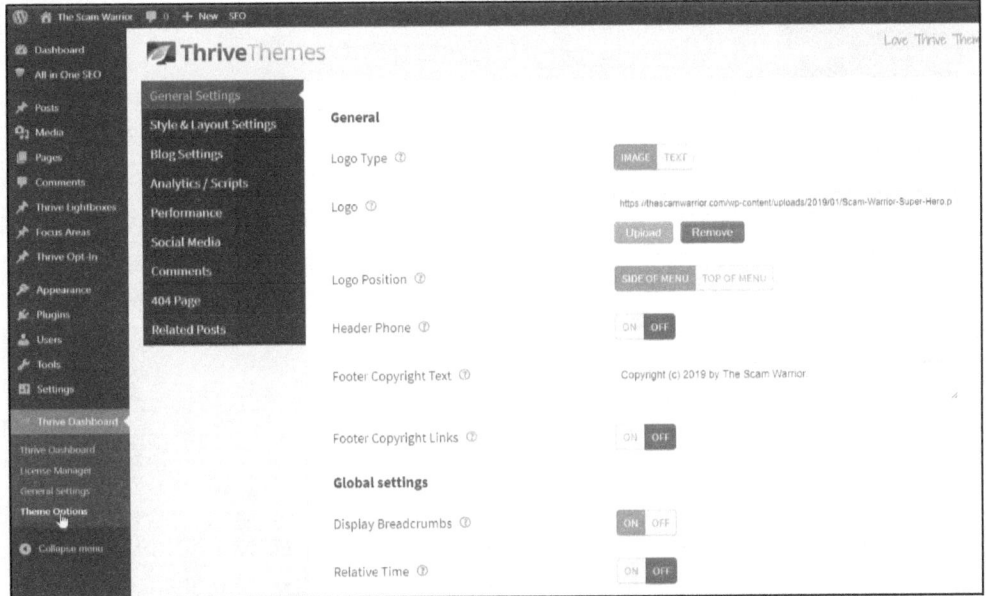

Figure 24: Thrive Theme Options

In your WordPress menu, select *Thrive Dashboard* then *Theme Options*.

Performance

In *Performance*, set *Image Optimization* to *Lossy Compression*. This should be done before any images are uploaded to your Media Library.

WordPress

for the Technically Challenged

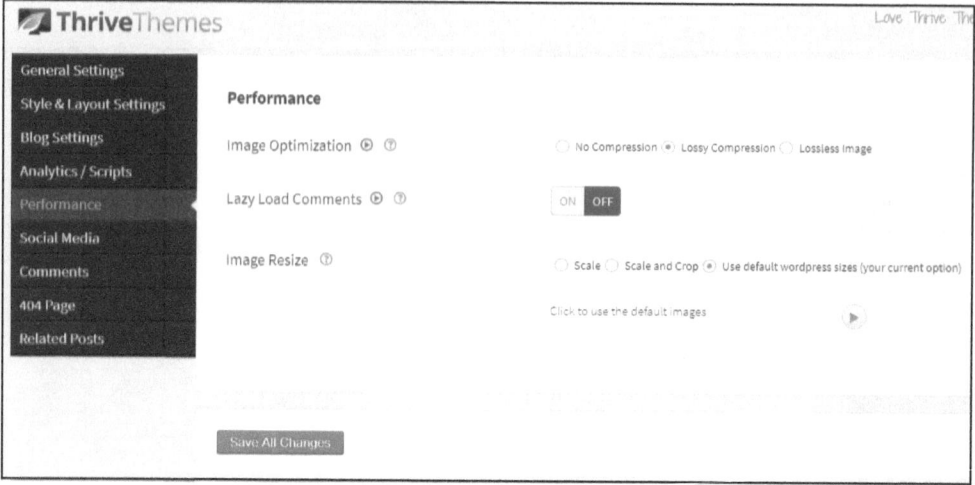

Figure 25: Performance

This setting makes no difference to image quality that can be detected by the human eye, but considerably reduces image size, resulting in faster loading of pages with images.

Click on *Save All Changes*.

In *General Settings*:

Set up Your Logo

Set Logo Type to Image, then under Logo, click *Upload* and select the file you are going to use as your logo.

Set the Logo Position to the side or the top of the menu, according to which is going to look best. This generally depends on the size of the logo and how many menu items you have. Note that we will set the actual logo size to be used elsewhere.

In the copyright message change "text" to © or "(c)".

To type the copyright symbol, make sure NumLk is on, hold down the Alt key and type 0169 using the numeric keypad. When you let the Alt key go, the copyright symbol will appear.

Footer Copyright Links

Set Footer Copyright Links to OFF.

Click on *Save All Changes*.

Style and Layout Settings

In *Style and Layout Settings*, insert Custom CSS that governs the size and style of fonts used for headings and paragraphs, as well as a couple of other things.

Putting it here means that it's not affected when the theme is updated.

WordPress

for the Technically Challenged

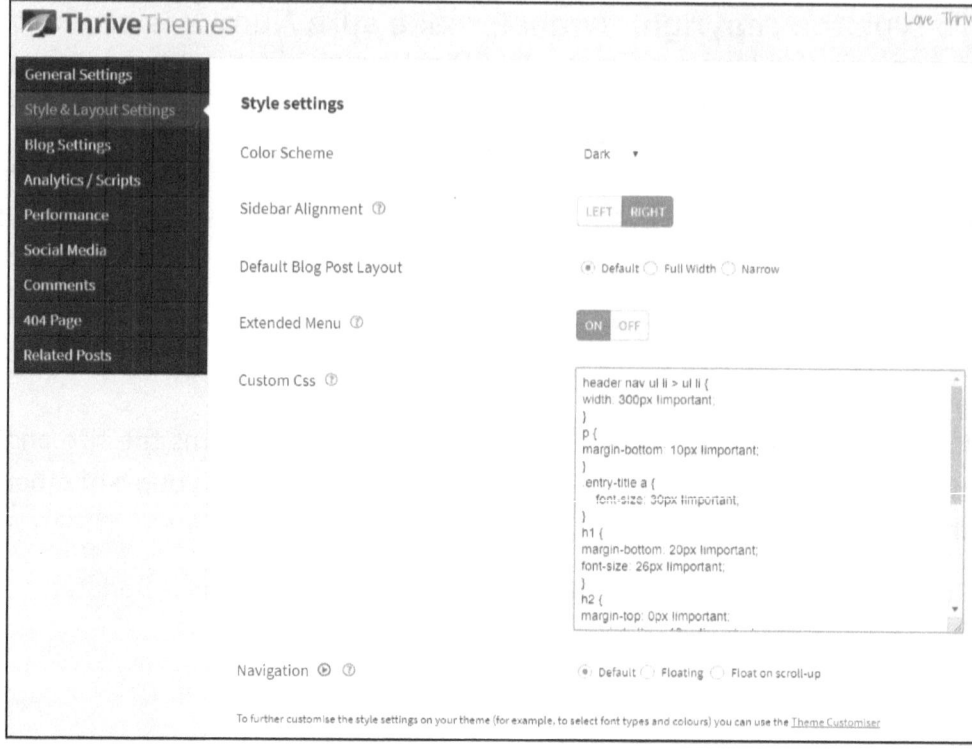

Figure 26: Style and Layout Settings

You should be able to copy and paste it from here.

```
header nav ul li > ul li {
width: 300px !important;
}
p {
margin-bottom: 10px !important;
}
.entry-title a {
    font-size: 30px !important;
}
h1 {
```

```
margin-bottom: 20px !important;
font-size: 26px !important;
}
h2 {
margin-top: 0px !important;
margin-bottom: 10px !important;
font-size: 22px !important;
}
h3 {
margin-top: 0px !important;
margin-bottom: 10px !important;
font-size: 18px !important;
}
p {
font-size:16px !important;
font-family : Literata, Verdana !important;
}
```

Click on *Save All Changes*.

Blog Settings

Make these changes in *Blog Settings*:

- Set Featured Image Style to *No Image*. This is because you don't want the featured image to appear in individual blog posts, but you do want it for a fabulous Thrive element called Post List, which I'll cover later.
- Set Post Category OFF. I just think posts look cleaner without them.
- Set Display Links to Previous and Next Posts ON. It helps keep visitors on your site.
- Show Read More as *Button*. This is what appears after the More… tag in your post.

WordPress

for the Technically Challenged

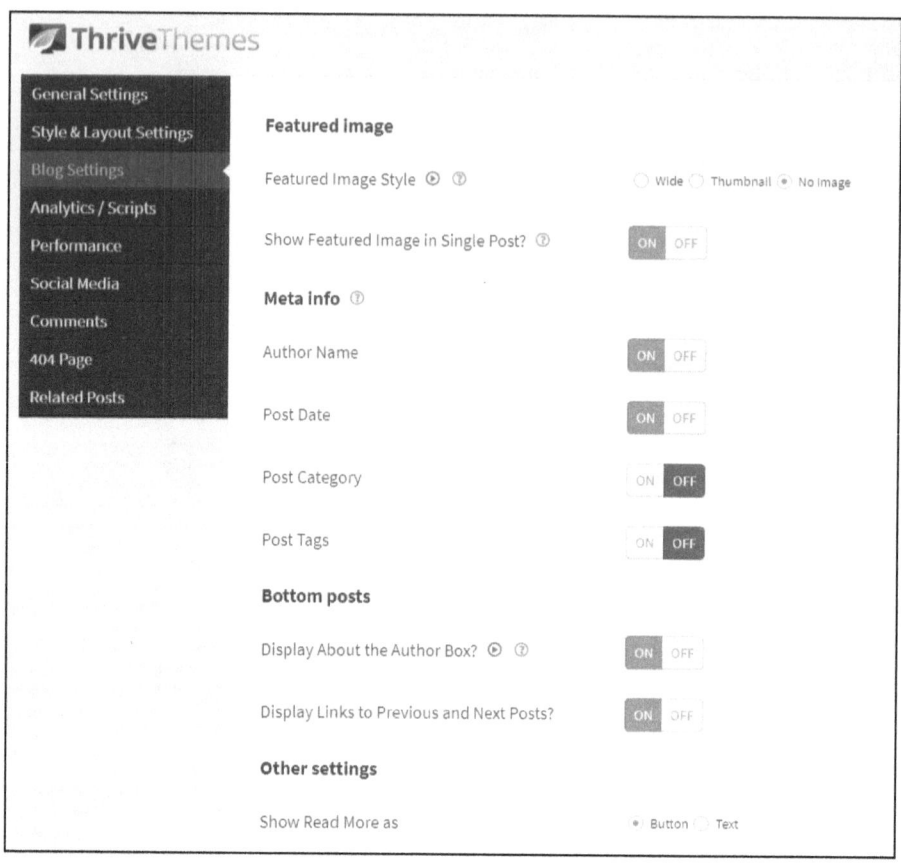

Figure 27: Blog Settings

Click on *Save All Changes*.

Analytics and Scripts is where you can enter scripts required by third parties, such as Google Analytics, Bing or Facebook.

WordPress
for the Technically Challenged

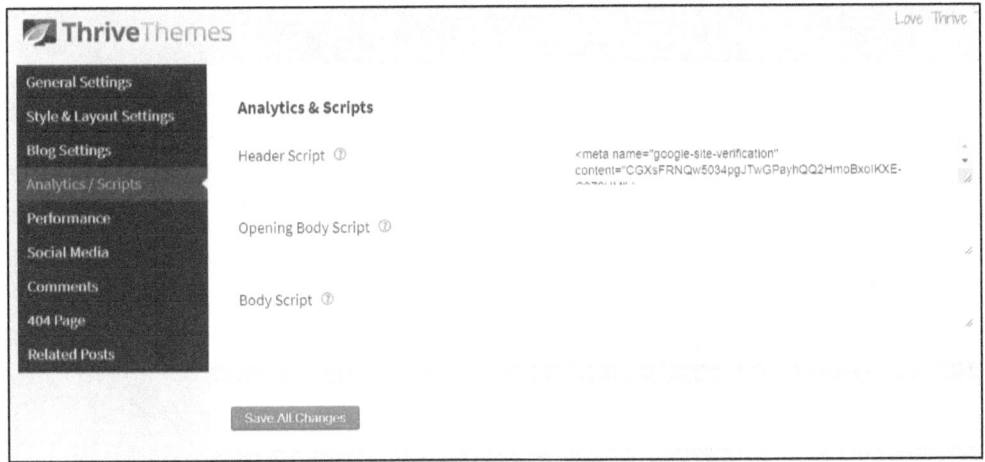

Figure 28: Analytics and Scripts

Set Logo Size

To set the logo size, from the WP side menu, select *Appearance >> Customize >> Header*.

WordPress

for the Technically Challenged

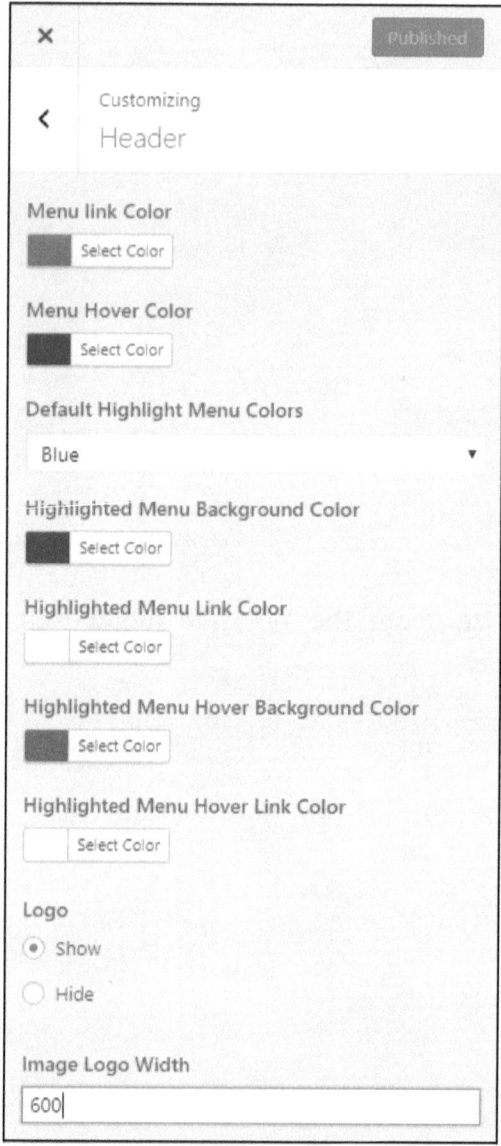

Figure 29: Customize Logo Width

WordPress

As you adjust the size of the logo, you will see the effect on your site, so you can get it just right.

Click the down-arrow next to Header Type and select Custom Color. Select white as the header color.

Click *Publish* when you're done.

Then click on the back arrow next to Customizing Header and select white as the background color.

Click *Publish* when you're done.

With the Luxe theme, this gives a very clean look.

Protecting Email Addresses

Some pages we will be adding will contain email addresses. These need to be hidden from email harvesting bots but still be human readable.

In the WordPress back office, go to Plugins >> Add Plugin, then search for Email Encoder and install it.

WordPress

for the Technically Challenged

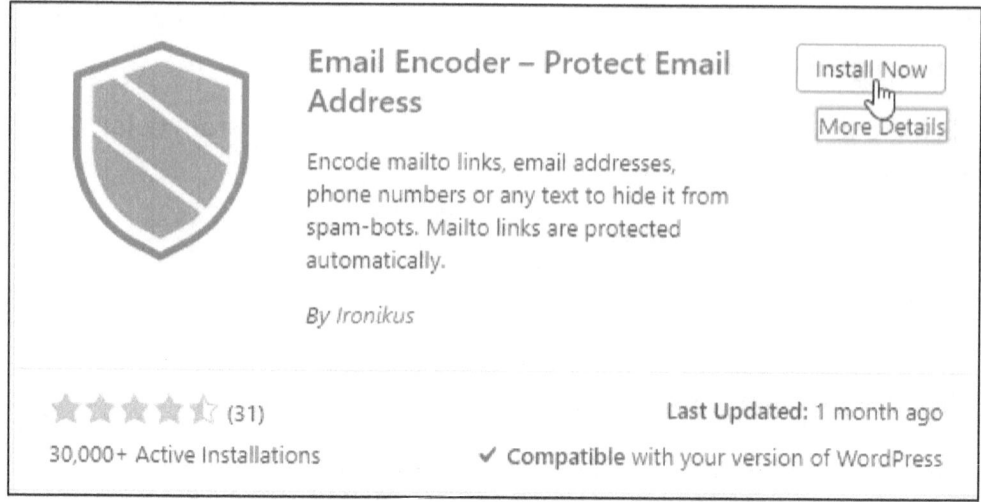

Figure 30: Install Email Encoder

Activate the plugin once it's been installed.

That's it. Your email addresses on posts and pages are now protected.

Adding a New User to Your WordPress Site

There are many reasons why you might want to add a new user to your WordPress site and to select a particular role for them.

You may have a friend, partner or business colleague who will contribute to your site and so you may wish to add them as an Editor.

But there is one person you should add as soon as your site is created, and that's YOU!

When your new, empty site is created it will have one administrator, usually named Admin and with an associated password. This is how you will initially log into your site.

WordPress

But a sure sign of an amateurish website is one where all the posts are by Admin and are Uncategorized.

You need to own your site and stamp your personality onto it. This is how you add yourself as a user.

Select Add New

In your WordPress back office, hover the mouse pointer over *Users*, then select *Add New*.

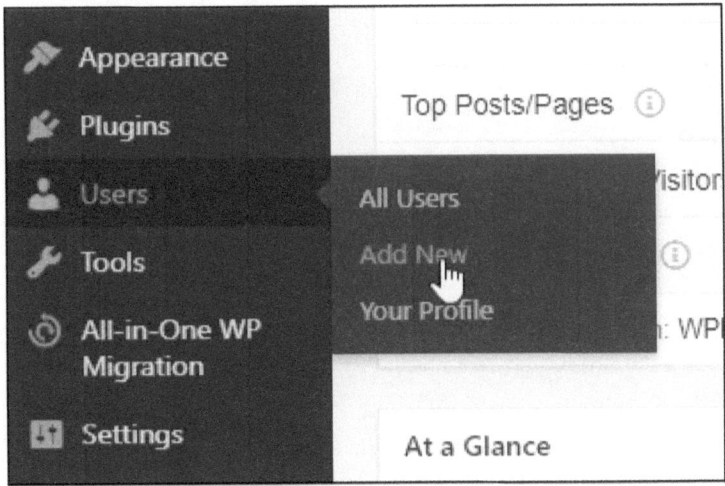

Figure 31: Select Add New

This will bring up the Add New User form.

WordPress
for the Technically Challenged

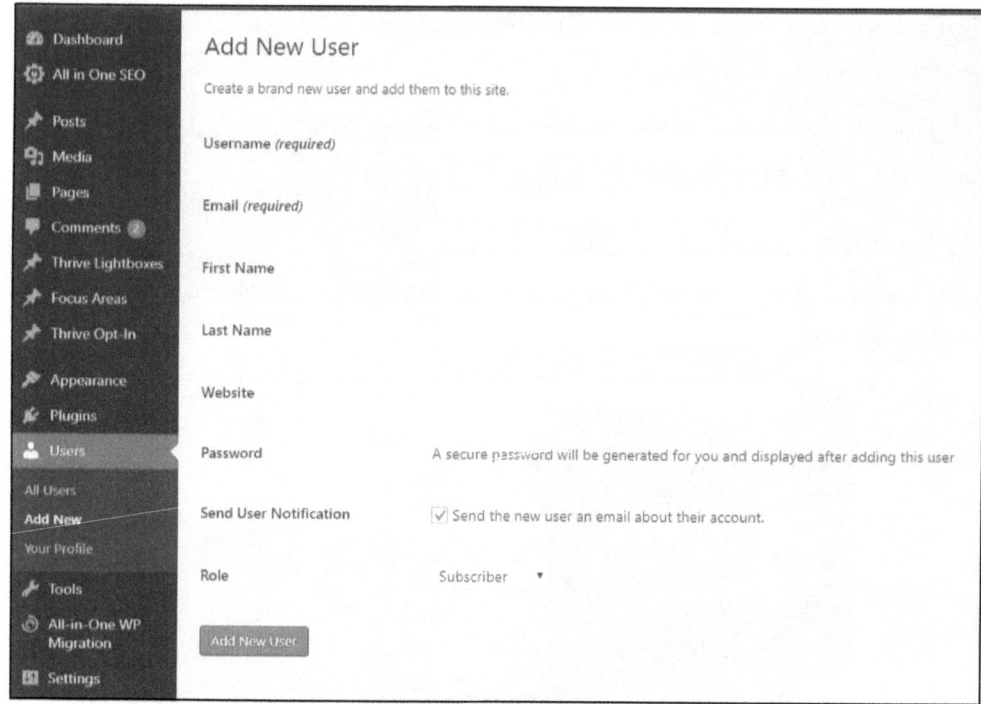

Figure 32: Add New User Form

Complete the Add New User Form
Then complete all the fields as follows:

Username	You can use anything you like, but I suggest your own first name.
Email	A valid email address of yours. No one else will see this, but your password will be sent here. It's useful if a Gravatar is associated with this email address. If you don't know what a Gravatar is, don't worry about it at this stage. You can set it up later.
First Name	Your first name.

44

WordPress

for the Technically Challenged

Last Name	Your last name.
Website	This website.
Password	Will be generated automatically.
Send User Notification	Leave this ticked.
Role	Click the drop-down and select Administrator.

Add New User

Create a brand new user and add them to this site.

Username (required)	Emma
Email (required)	emma@newyeardetox.com.au
First Name	Emma
Last Name	Morgan
Website	https://superaffiliatechallenge.com
Password	A secure password will be generated for you and displayed after adding this user
Send User Notification	☑ Send the new user an email about their account.
Role	Administrator ▾

Add New User

Figure 33: The Completed Add New User Form

Add the New User

Click the **Add New User** button when everything is complete.

WordPress

for the Technically Challenged

Save the generated password when prompted to do so, after displaying it and copying it to a safe location.

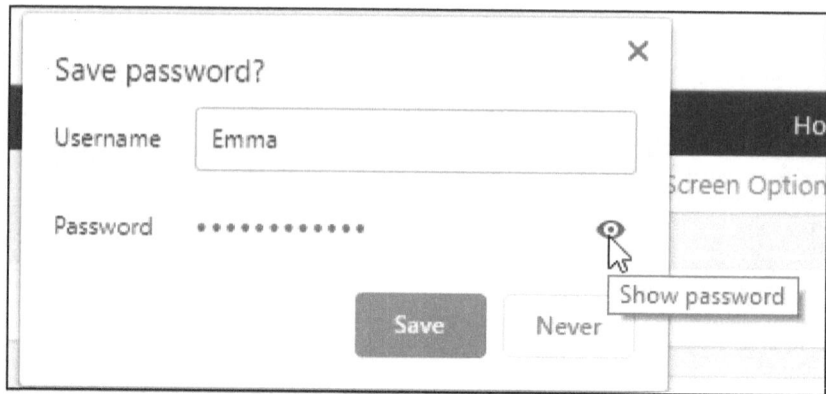

Figure 34: Save the Generated Password

Note that you can click on the little eye icon to display the password. You should copy and save it in a safe place.

For example, I keep all my passwords in a memorized password-protected Word document. There are also a number of secure password storage apps available.

You will see that your new user has been added.

WordPress

for the Technically Challenged

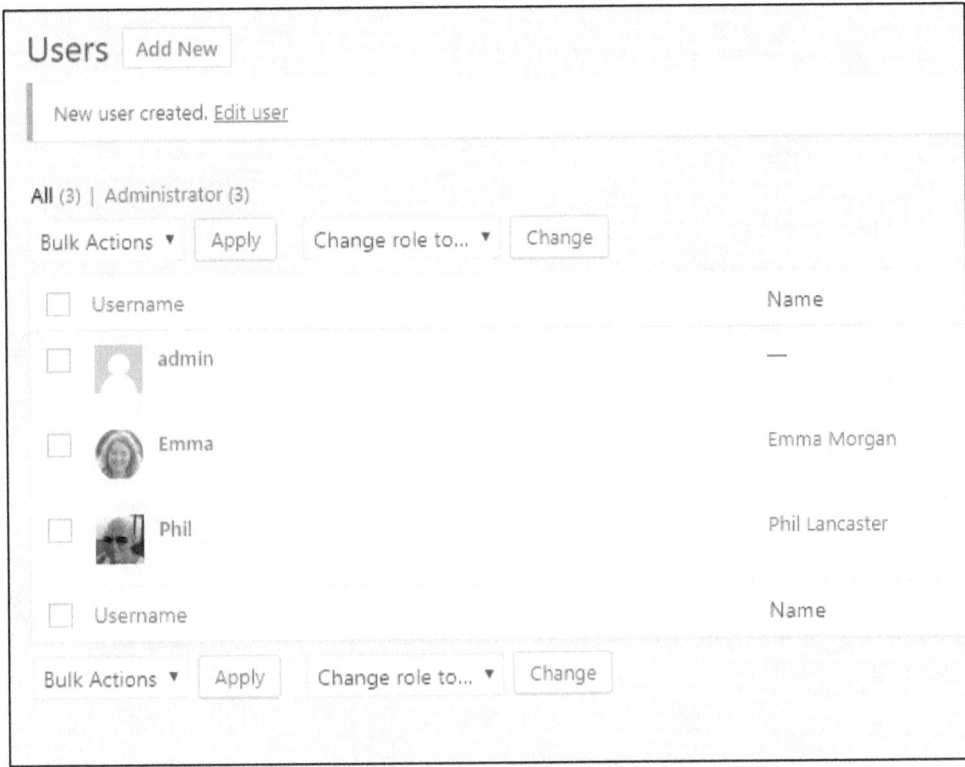

Figure 35: New User Created

Note that Emma's image has appeared automatically. That's because her email address and image are registered with Gravatar.

Check the WordPress Email

WordPress automatically sends an email to the new user at the email address entered. This can be used to change the password if desired.

WordPress

for the Technically Challenged

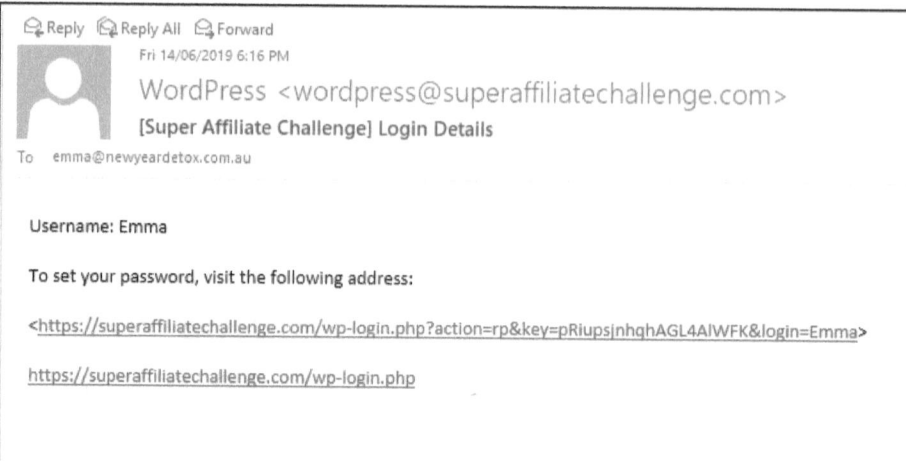

Figure 36: Password Email

If you choose this option, the password will be reset to a new secure password which will be displayed on screen for you to copy and store securely.

WordPress

Figure 37: Password Reset from Email

Log in with the New User's Credentials

The new user can log into the website at domainname/wp-admin with the new username and password.

Logging in at https://superaffiliatechallenge.com/wp-admin

WordPress

Figure 38: Log in as the New User

WordPress will show that the new user is logged in.

WordPress

for the Technically Challenged

The New User Is Logged in

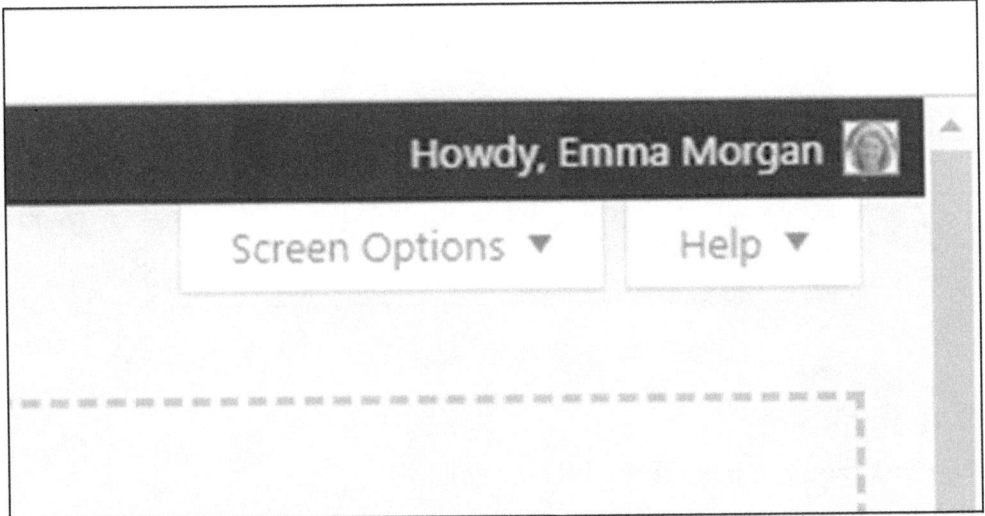

Figure 39: Logged in as the New User

Now any new posts or pages will be attributed to the new user.

Adding Required Pages and Posts

You will need to add a Privacy Policy and an Affiliate Disclosure. If you Google these two terms, you will find samples you can use. They may require some modification to suit the style of your website.

I suggest you store them in a Word document so that you can copy and paste them into your website(s) easily.

To add a page, hover over Pages in the WordPress back office, then click on *Add New*.

WordPress

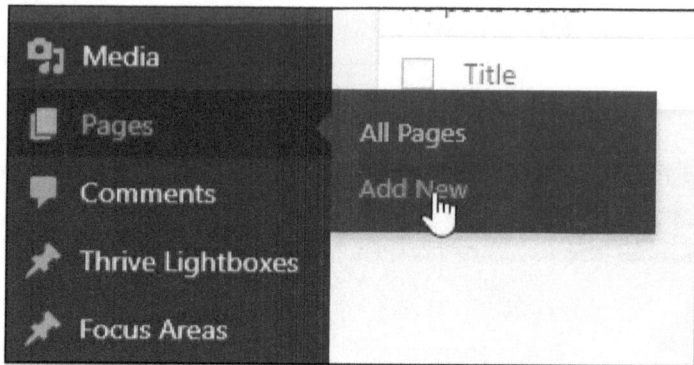

Figure 40: Click on Add New (Page)

Privacy Policy

The first required page is the Privacy Policy.

Enter the name of the page as Privacy Policy, scroll down and also enter the Title as Privacy Policy, then click on the **Save Draft** button on the right-hand side.

Then click on the **Launch Thrive Architect** button.

WordPress

for the Technically Challenged

Figure 41: Launch Thrive Architect

Once Thrive Architect has been launched, click on the Elements icon (it's the square box with a plus sign in it) on the right-hand side and select the Text element.

WordPress

for the Technically Challenged

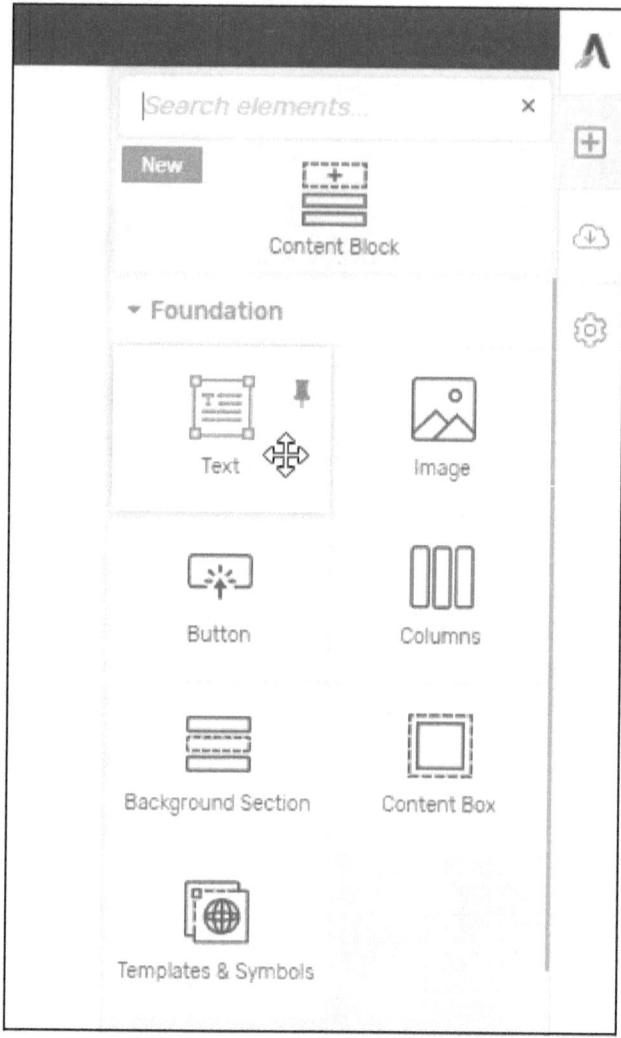

Figure 42: Add a Thrive Architect Text Element

This will open a text box on your page.

Copy and paste your privacy policy from your Word document into the text box.

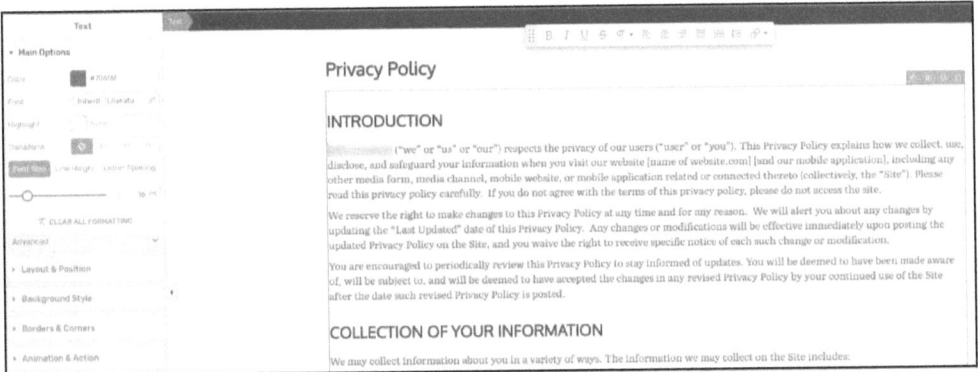

Figure 43: Privacy Policy Pasted into Text Box

Then click on the **Save Work** button.

Note that the page is still a draft. To publish it, close the Thrive Architect screen, then click on the page name back in the WordPress back office. From here, you can click the **Publish** button.

WordPress

for the Technically Challenged

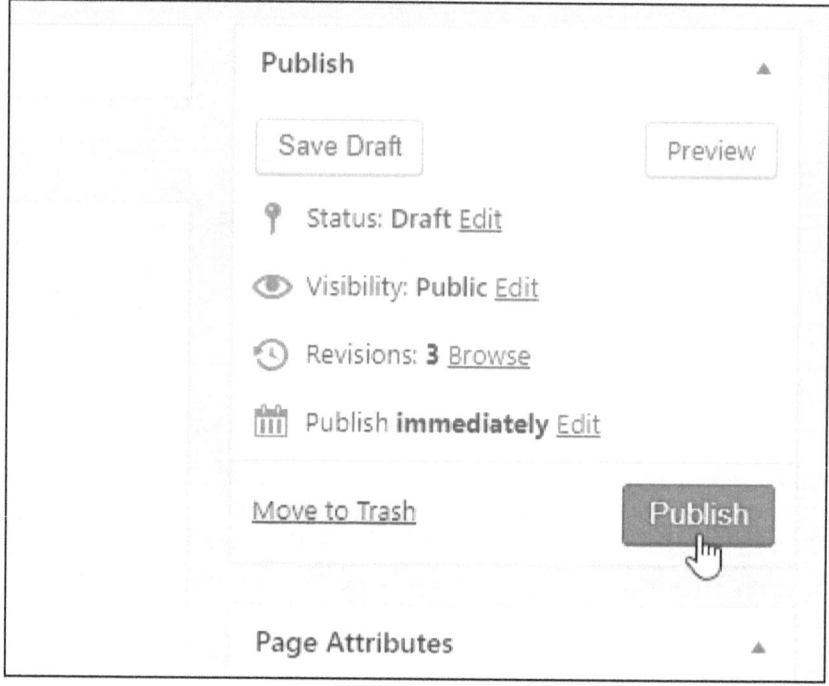

Figure 44: Publish the Page

Affiliate Disclosure

Create your Affiliate Disclosure page in exactly the same way as your Privacy Policy page and publish it.

Articles

The Articles page is very simple to create but very powerful. It will automatically show all of your blog posts (articles) making them all accessible in the one place and doubling their exposure.

Create an empty page, using Articles as the page name and the title, save it as a draft and launch Thrive Architect.

WordPress

for the Technically Challenged

The Post List Element

Figure 45: The Post List Element

The Post List element is incredibly powerful, delivering an impressive result for almost no work.

It can be used in many ways, but I'll give you one example and then you can experiment to get your own desired result.

I've created a new page called Articles and added it to my main menu.

The only thing on the page is a Post List element.

WordPress

for the Technically Challenged

Figure 46: Post List Element Added to Articles Page

The idea of the Post List element is to display any or all of your posts and pages in a grid pattern over which you have total control

I'm going to set mine up to display all posts in a 3 across grid, with the latest first, illustrated by the featured image, showing an excerpt and a Read More... tag.

The beauty is that once it's set up, new posts will automatically be added to it. No further attention is required.

Click on *Post List*, then *Edit Design*.

WordPress

for the Technically Challenged

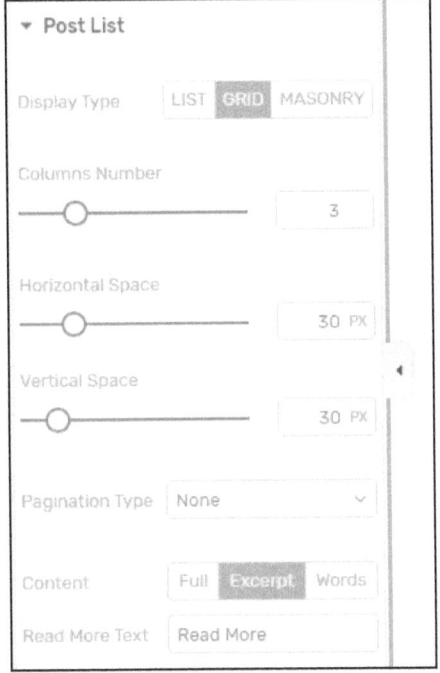

Figure 47: Post List Design

Here you can set:

Display Type	I use Grid
Number of Columns	I use 3
Content	I use Excerpt
Read More Text	I use "Read More"

Then click the **DONE** button.

Back under Post List, click Filter Posts.

WordPress
for the Technically Challenged

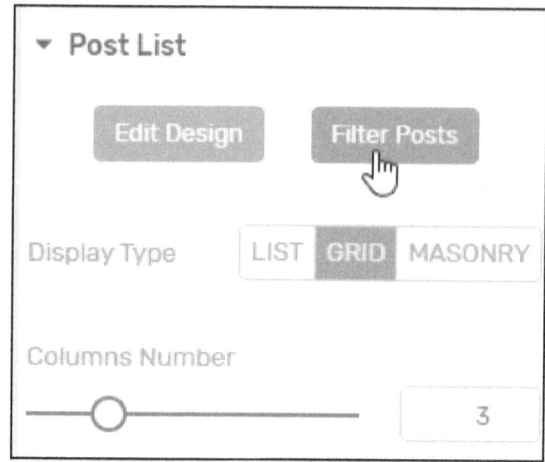

Figure 48: Filter Posts

Then set parameters for the posts to be displayed.

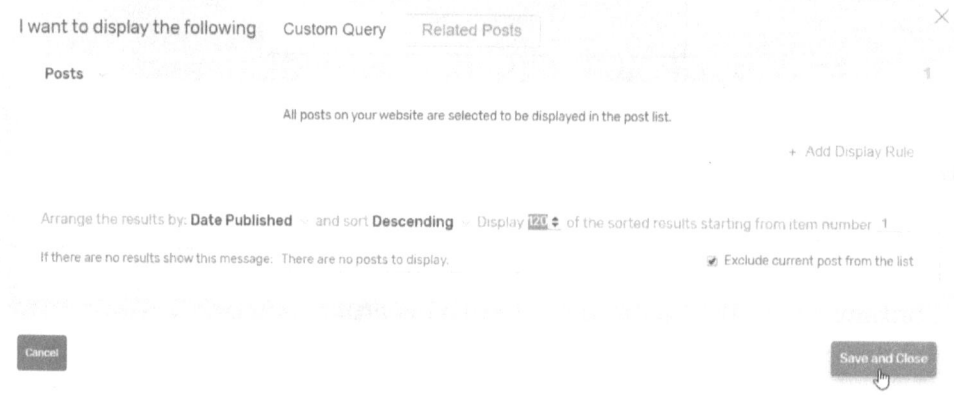

Figure 49: Select the Posts to be Displayed

If you simply want to display a large number of recent posts, set the number to be displayed and leave everything else.

WordPress

for the Technically Challenged

Figure 50: The Finished Articles Page

And that's it. With minimal work, I have a page that shows all my blog articles as soon as they're posted, nicely laid out and with a link to the full article.

Note that pages can be displayed in exactly the same manner. This can be an easy way of displaying groups of products by category.

WordPress

That's it! Click Done then Save Work. Exit Thrive Architect and publish the page.

About (Me)

There are two more required pieces of information, but you will do these as posts, rather than pages. This is to allow visitors to comment on them.

The first one is the About (Me) post. I you prefer, you can substitute your own name for (Me) so that it's more personal.

Creating a post is similar to creating a page.

To add a post, hover over Posts in the WordPress back office, then click on *Add New*. Or click on Posts and then the **Add New** button.

Figure 51: Click the Add New (Post) Button

Just as for adding a page, enter the name About (Me) scroll down and enter it in the Title as well.

Unlike pages, posts need to be categorized.

WordPress

for the Technically Challenged

On the right-hand side of the draft post, you will see Categories, Tags and Featured Image. Click on *Add New Category*.

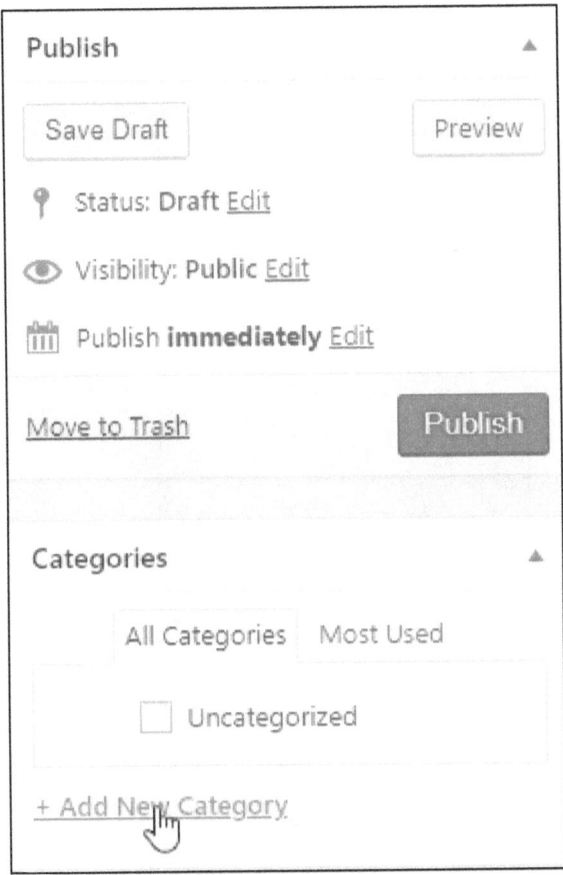

Figure 52: Add New Category

Enter About Me into the text box and click on the **Add New Category** button.

The new category should have a check mark against it and uncategorized should be unchecked.

WordPress

Then scroll down to *Set Featured Image* and upload a nice photo of yourself. The ideal size is 400 px by 400 px.

Click on the **Save Draft** button and then *Launch Thrive Architect*.

Select the Image element from the right-hand side.

Figure 53: Select the Image Element

WordPress

You will be prompted to choose an image from your media library. Your photo will have been uploaded when you chose it as your featured image, so select it now and click on the **Insert into Post** button.

Click on the inserted image. Its properties will appear on the left-hand side.

WordPress

for the Technically Challenged

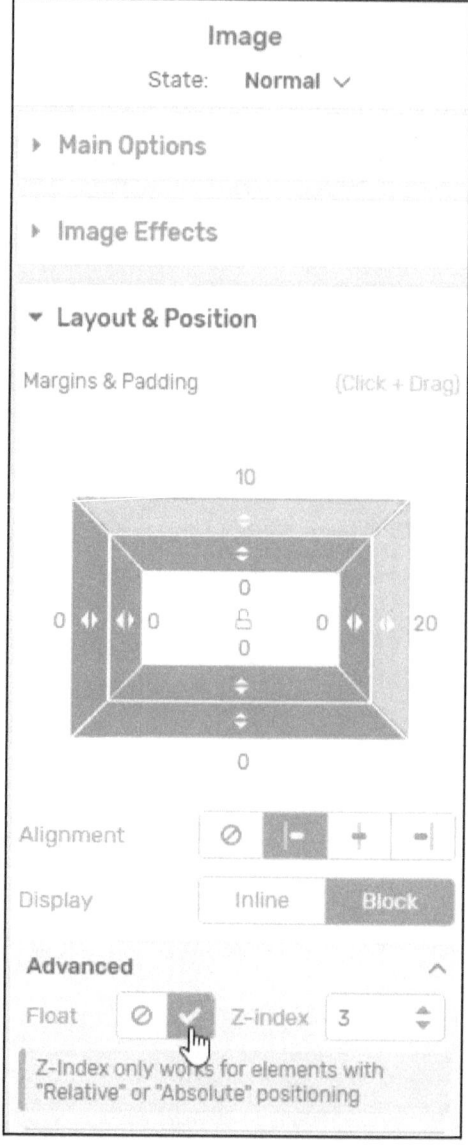

Figure 54: Set the Image Properties

We need to make some changes to the image's properties.

Under *Main Options*, check the size and adjust it if necessary, to 400 px.

Under *Layout & Position* (shown above) change the top margin to 10, the right-hand margin to 20 and the bottom margin to 0.

Click on the left alignment icon, and under *Advanced*, click the Float checkmark.

This will cause the following text to float nicely around the image.

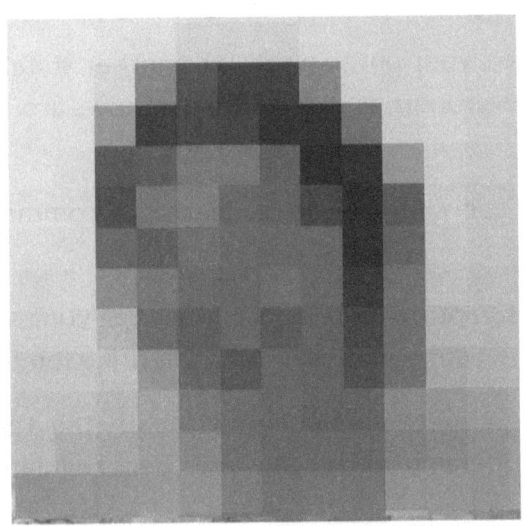

About

Lorem ipsum dolor sit amet, nam consulatu efficiantur mediocritatem et, ad atqui homero feugait eum. Consul integre intellegebat eu quo, ne eam diam consul. Ad pro dissentias complectitur. Nam omnis illum gubergren at, qui eu amet audire corpora. Brute imperdiet abhorreant et sea, enim iriure cu duo. Cu diam salutandi assentior vel, cum virtute splendide ne, pri ne luptatum ullamcorper.

Vivendum conceptam percipitur eum ut, te wisi virtute delenit cum. Affert reprimique ne sit, per fugit tacimates qualisque at. Eam an brute movet option. Facilis euripidis ex sit, melius inimicus assentior ex usu, eam ea stet congue. Eam eu eius adolescens. Ea etiam populo usu.

Liber liberavisse mei no. Offendit delicatissimi per at, vero latine blandit his an. Illud tincidunt cu pro. Modo impetus placerat ad pri. Vel mutat harum nihil ex, in assum omittantur nam, ut complectitur mediocritatem cum. Vis ei quodsi convenire, brute zril ocurreret ne eum, sit ei reformidans philosophia.

Figure 55: About Me Page with Placeholder Text

Then click on Save Work, close the Thrive Architect page and publish the post.

Contact (Me)

The second required post is the Contact (Me) post. Substitute your own name for (Me) so that it's more personal.

The purpose of this post is simply to create a space on your website where a visitor can easily contact you leaving a comment.

Proceed as for the About (Me) post (using Contact Me as the new category) until you've got a new page with Thrive Architect loaded.

As for the About (Me) post, insert your photograph (or another suitable image) as an image and modify its properties so that the text flows around it.

Enter some text that says they can contact you by leaving a comment below.

It looks good if you can put your signature underneath. A scan of your real signature is best. Failing that, type your name using a handwriting font.

Insert a Contact Form Thrive Architect element underneath the text, setting the email address to one that you will receive and check regularly.

Contact Me

I love hearing from my visitors and always reply as quickly as I can.

Please use the comment form below to get in touch with me.

If you have any comments about the site or any questions about dogs or other pets, just let me know and I'll answer as completely and honestly as I can.

If I need advice, I can always ask my best friend and companion, my black labrador ▪ .

First Name

John

Email Address

j.doe@inbox.com

Message

Type your message here...

Figure 56: Contact (Me) Post

Go back to the WordPress back office and click *Publish* to publish your new post.

WordPress

for the Technically Challenged

Creating Your Menus

You will create two menus, a header menu to be shown at the top of each page and a footer menu to be shown at the bottom.

In the WordPress back office, click on Appearance then Menus.

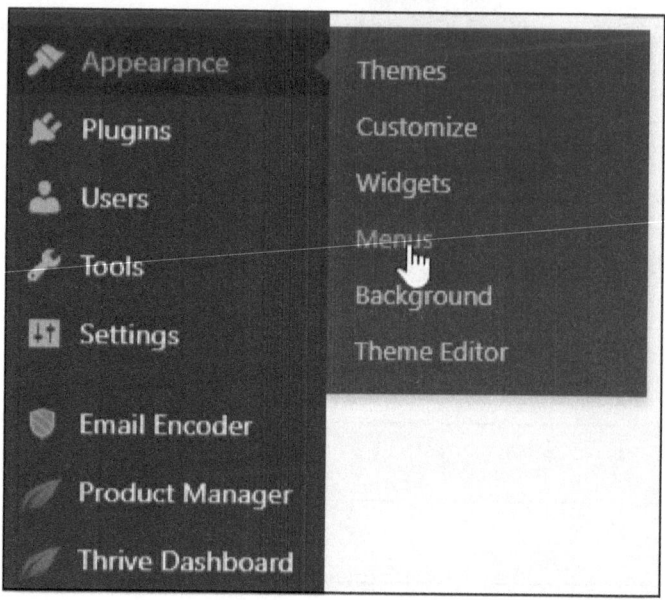

Figure 57: Select Appearance then Menus

Give your menu a name, such as Header Menu and click on *Create Menu*.

Figure 58: Create Your Header Menu

Under *Menu Settings*, set Location to Primary Menu.

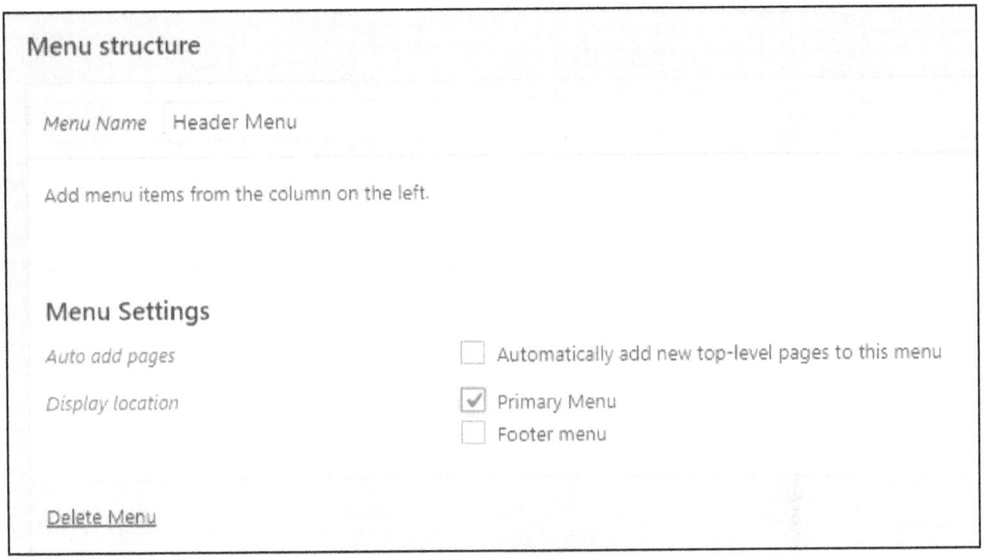

WordPress

for the Technically Challenged

Menu structure

Menu Name   Header Menu

Add menu items from the column on the left.

Menu Settings

Auto add pages   ☐ Automatically add new top-level pages to this menu

Display location   ☑ Primary Menu
                        ☐ Footer menu

Delete Menu

Figure 59: Set Location to Primary Menu

Then click the **Save Menu** button.

The first menu item you will add is HOME.

Under Add Menu Items, click on *Custom Links*, enter your site's URL and HOME as the link text.

WordPress

for the Technically Challenged

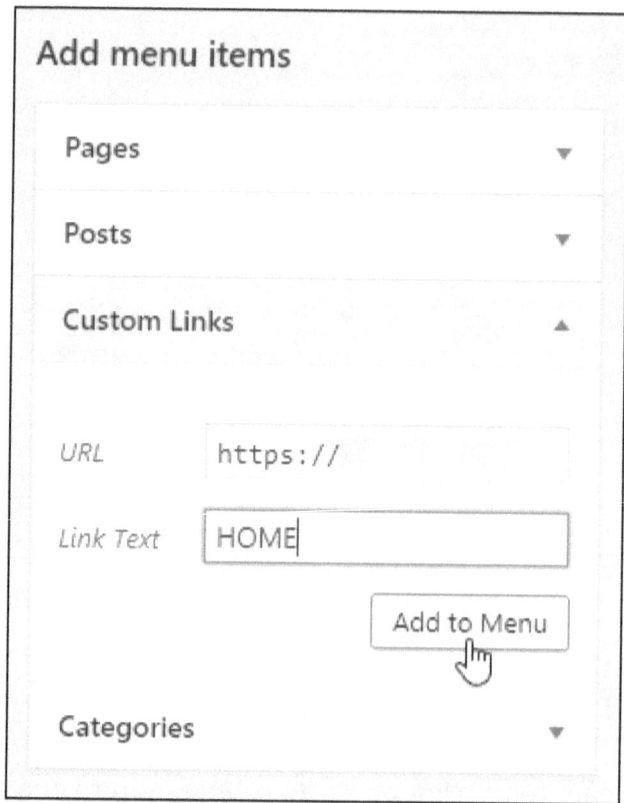

Figure 60: Create the Home Menu Item

Click on the **Add to Menu** button.

Then open Pages, click Articles and Privacy Policy to checkmark them and click on the **Add to Menu** button.

Under Menu Structure, click on the drop-downs next to each of the new menu items and change the navigation label to upper case (it just looks better on a menu).

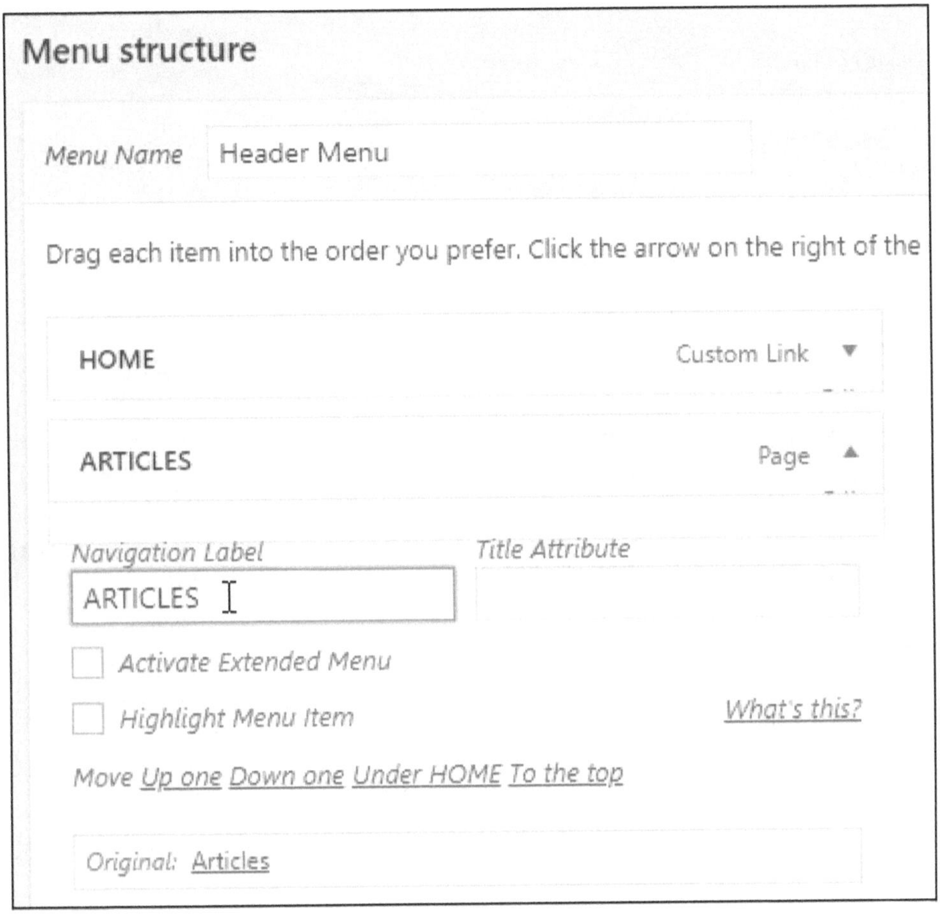

WordPress

for the Technically Challenged

Menu structure

Menu Name   Header Menu

Drag each item into the order you prefer. Click the arrow on the right of the

HOME   Custom Link ▼

ARTICLES   Page ▲

Navigation Label   Title Attribute

ARTICLES I

☐ Activate Extended Menu

☐ Highlight Menu Item   What's this?

Move Up one Down one Under HOME To the top

Original: Articles

Figure 61: Change the Menu Item Name to Upper Case

Go back to Add Menu Items, click on Posts and add the Contact (Me) and About (Me) posts to the menu. Change the navigation labels to upper case.

Click the **Save Menu** button and your header menu is done!

Now to create your Footer Menu. It will contain just two items, your Privacy Policy and your Affiliate Disclosure.

WordPress
for the Technically Challenged

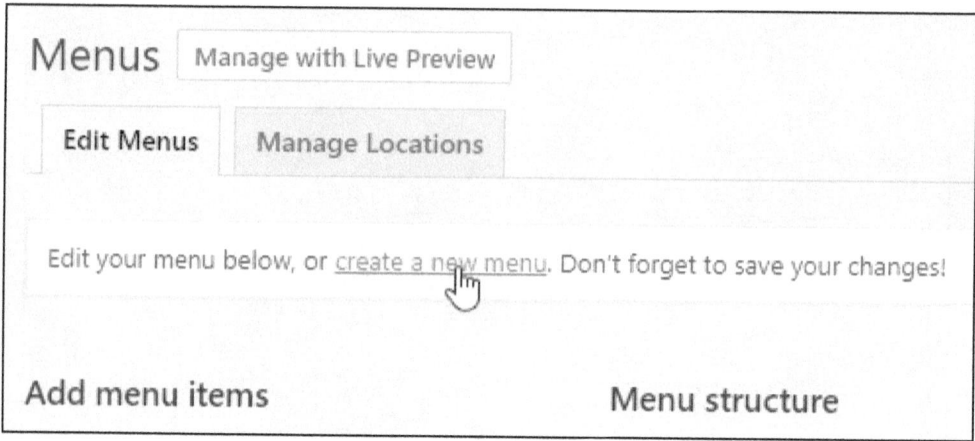

Figure 62: Select Create a New Menu

Give your new menu the name Footer Menu and click on the **Create Menu** button.

Select Footer Menu as the Location.

Menu structure

Menu Name Footer Menu

Add menu items from the column on the left.

Menu Settings

Auto add pages ☐ Automatically add new top-level pages to this menu

Display location ☐ Primary Menu (Currently set to: Header Menu)
☑ Footer menu

Delete Menu

Figure 63: Select Footer Menu as the Location

WordPress

Add the pages Affiliate Disclosure and Privacy Policy to the menu. The Luxe theme will automatically make them upper case, so you can skip that step.

Click on the **Save Menu** button and you're done.

Your WordPress Site Is Ready!

Go to your website and check everything out.

Other Plugins

Here are some other plugins that you will find useful.

To add them to your website, go to Plugins >> Add New then search for them by name, install and activate.

WordPress

for the Technically Challenged

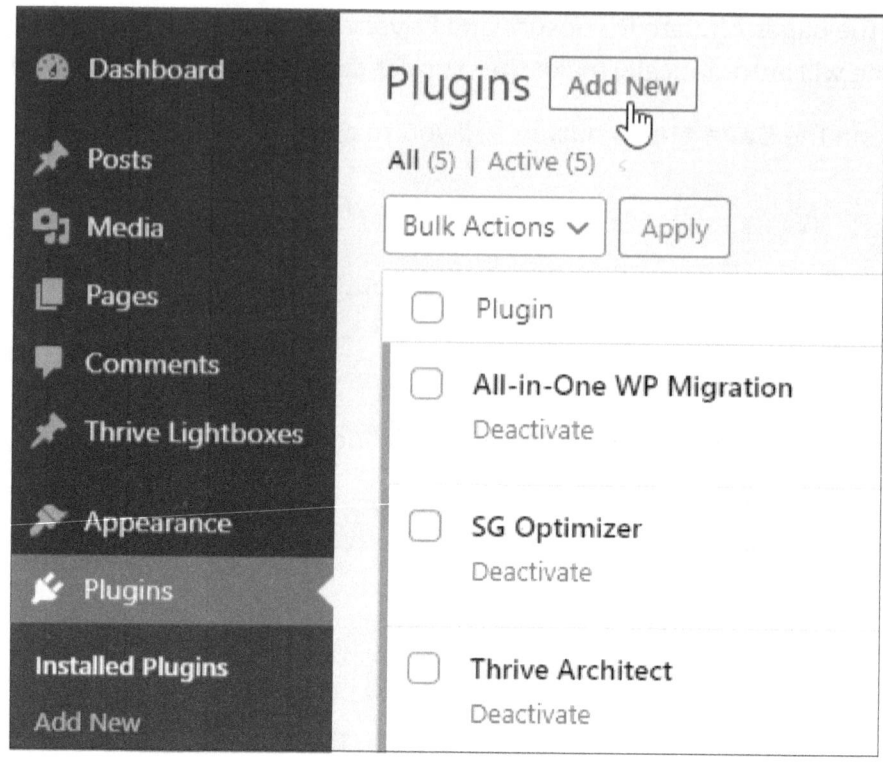

Figure 64: Add a New Plugin

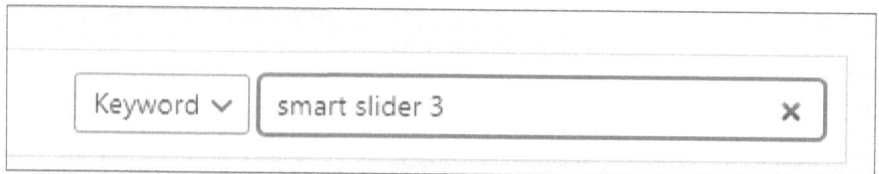

Figure 65: Search for the Plugin You Want

WordPress

for the Technically Challenged

Figure 66: Install and Activate the New Plugin

All-in-One SEO Pack

This plugin improves your search engine optimization and allows you to generate a Google-friendly XML site map.

All-in-One WP Migration

This plugin allows easy backup and restore of your entire website. Not only does it protect you against losing data, but it can be used to transfer from one web host to another.

Monster Insights

You have to have Google Analytics running for your website first but then Monster Insights displays essential analytical data directly on your website.

Under Construction

If you are working on your website and don't want it to be visible right now, this plugin allows a simple switch between site available or not. You have a number of templates to choose from.

WordPress

for the Technically Challenged

Figure 67: Under Construction Enabled

Smart Slider 3

This plugin creates a slide show of images.

For an example of this used to create a slide show header, have a look at my Driven by Golf website https://drivenbygolf.com.

AliDropship

All of the above plugins are free, but you have to pay for AliDropship.

78

WordPress

You only need it if you are running an e-commerce store and sourcing products from AliExpress.

The AliDropship plugin imports selected products directly from AliExpress, including images, descriptions and prices. Prices are marked up according to how much profit you wish to make.

When your customer gives you an order and pays, AliDropship creates the corresponding order on the supplier internally, so that all you have to do is approve it. It's a massive time saver for e-commerce businesses.

You can check out AliDropship at https://alidropship.com/?via=12851.

WordPress

for the Technically Challenged

The Rest of the Books

Here are all the books in my Internet Marketing FAST series, all available as Kindle Singles.

Available Now

1. The 4 Things You Must Know (to Make Money While You Sleep)
2. How to Select Your Internet Marketing Niche
3. How to Register a Domain Name
4. How to Host Your Website
5. WordPress for the Technically Challenged
6. Building Your Website with Thrive
7. The Thrive User
8. The Thrive Expert

Not Yet Available

9. Become an Affiliate Marketing Ninja
10. Become an E-Commerce Ninja
11. The Deadly Combo of Blog Posts and Landing Pages
12. Google is Your New Best Friend
13. Building Your Mailing List
14. All About Free and Paid Traffic
15. How to Publish Your Book on Amazon
16. The Secret to Making Money with Your Internet Businesses (after You've Done Everything Else)

You can get the Kindle and Paperback links to the books on Amazon at

WordPress

for the Technically Challenged

https://superaffiliatechallenge.com/internet-marketing-fast-books-from-amazon/

WordPress

for the Technically Challenged

About the Author

As an 80 year old (in2024) fitness fanatic and successful internet marketer, Phil Lancaster is a bit of an anomaly.

Through a combination of bad luck and bad business decisions, he found himself broke and alone at 74.

Now, a few years later, he has several internet businesses that combine to bring him a 6-figure income.

It wasn't easy and he got burned a few times on the way, but he reckons that anyone can do it with the right road map.

He wants to help you to get started the way he did, but without making the same mistakes.

Anyone, from student to baby boomer (and older) can make money through the internet.

Phil's IM Fast series of mini-books will get you started. At just $2.99 each, you won't find a better investment.

www.ingramcontent.com/pod-product-compliance
Lightning Source LLC
Chambersburg PA
CBHW020606220526
45463CB00006B/2477